RAPE

by Carol V. Horos

A Dell/Banbury Book

Published by
Banbury Books, Inc.
37 West Avenue
Wayne, Pennsylvania 19087

Dell ® TM 681510, Dell Publishing Co., Inc.

ISBN: 0-440-07216-6

Reprinted by arrangement with Tobey Publishing Co., Inc.
Printed in the United States of America
First Dell/Banbury printing—March 1981

Table of Contents

RAPE

Introduction

Throughout history women have been in the vanguard of movements for justice and change. We have been the nurses, the helpers, the listeners, the millions who swelled the ranks of every movement in history—and we are proud of it! But finally our energies have come full circle. We can no longer accept fear as a way of life, we can no longer accept definitions of rape as a sexual encounter—rape is a crime of hate and violence, committed by a man who uses sex as a weapon to inflict violence on his victim. Women are beginning to recognize themselves as people, as human beings—proud to be women! It is this new-found pride that refuses to tolerate the dehumanizing crime of rape. We are developing a great community sense of outrage—and for women this is a wonderful new phenomenon. Because, in order to feel outrage, women must first think well of themselves.

We recognize not only the oppression of the crime of rape itself; we recognize the institutions and the individuals who support and encourage this oppression through ignorance—these are our courts, our hospitals, our legislatures, police, district attorneys and detectives.

A great number of women affected by the crime

of rape have no choice but to use the existing institutions involved in prosecuting this crime.
Whether it is through poor training, ignorance or
callousness, the experience of reporting rape is,
for most women, a trauma that often proves worse
than the rape itself. At present these institutions
exist like giants but they are giants that can't be
ignored—not as long as ONE woman is forced to
use them. We see these giants as compositions of
individuals—and therefore capable of change.

It remains for women, once again, to rise, to
swell the ranks, to bring about this change—and to
demand that Society join us!

Jody Pinto, founder
Women Organized Against Rape

1
The History of Rape: A Painful Perspective

Many of the prevailing attitudes toward rape are remnants from a past which had little or no consideration for women as people. The myths about rape are social commentaries on a woman's place in an ancient world, a world where she had no legal, social or human rights. Even though the status of women has evolved from possession to person, the myths remain the same. In fact, they are so well preserved, our modern laws are based on them.

The word "rape" is derived from the Latin *rapere*, meaning "to steal, seize or carry away." Rape is the oldest means by which a man seized or stole a wife. It was enforced marriage without the trappings of courtship. A man simply took whichever woman he wanted, raped her and then brought her into his tribe. She was little more than a trophy, living proof of his virility and one of the nicer by-products of the spoils of war.

Gradually forcible rape lost some of its respectability and the blame for certain rapes shifted to the victim. Herodotus, called the Father of History, commented on the subject in 500 B.C. To him, "Abducting young women is not, indeed, a lawful act; but it is stupid after the event to make a fuss about it. The only sensible thing is to take no notice; for it is obvious that no young woman allows herself to be abducted if she does not wish to be." It was that simple. If you were raped, you must have been looking for it.

When marriage evolved into a sanctioned institution of the tribe, forcible rape became a crime. Women were seen as property and property was valuable. If a man wanted a wife he was compelled by tribal law to buy her.

Under the law, every female was technically owned by her father. But when she married, the right of ownership passed from the father to the husband who had paid a sum of money for the privilege. In essence, a marriage contract was the same as changing the title on a car. A woman took the name of her husband because he held the property rights. She literally belonged to him. Therefore, any infringement or damage to his human property (rape) was, first and foremost, a direct offense against her husband and a crime against the community.

Society's view of rape was purely a matter of economics—of assets and liabilities. When a married woman was raped, her husband was wronged, not her. If she was unmarried, her father suffered since his investment depreciated. It was the monetary value of a woman which determined the gravity of the crime. Because she had no personal rights under the law, her own emotions simply didn't matter. The important reaction to rape was the man's reaction—"How could he (the rapist) do this to me?" Laws, justice and women belonged to the world of men. The victim was just a pawn swept along by circumstances over which she was powerless to contain or control.

RAPE AND THE VIRGIN

The difference between raping a married women and deflowering a virgin was like trying to equate a misdemeanor with a felony.

A virgin was believed to have supernatural powers, powers which were hers by virtue of her chastity. She possessed electrifying, God-given forces that could ward off evil spirits, cause the oceans and fields to be fertile and insure the blessings of the gods on her community. Everything that was magical, life-giving and good belonged to the virgin. She was a valuable commodity and her chastity was feared, revered and ruthlessly protected.

Raping a virgin was a heinous crime not only from the superstitious standpoint of incurring the wrath of the gods but also by the practical fact of lessening her price on the marriage market. Chastity was of the utmost importance in a marriage contract, similar to the importance of a warranty on an appliance. If for some reason the marriage didn't work, the prior unchastity of the woman was ample grounds for divorce. Also, men were reluctant to purchase (marry) second-hand or "used" women, since nonvirgins had obviously lost touch with the Almighty.

To rape a virgin was to commit mortal sin

while irreparably damaging precious merchandise. Babylonia and Assyria punished the hapless rapist by death (if he was married). However, economics were of the first concern and if you killed an unmarried rapist, who would marry the deflowered virgin? In these cases the rapist was forced to marry his victim and pay her father three times her original marriage price. In addition, the girl's father was allowed a "rape of retribution" which legally permitted him to rape the ravisher's wife or sister.

Biblical law banned all rapes of reprisal and instead, the man was obligated to marry his victim while paying her father no more than the traditional bride-price. As an added penalty the rapist could never divorce his victim. Once again, the woman's feelings fell by the wayside. She was forced to marry her rapist and to stay with him for the rest of her life.

THE CODE OF PUNISHMENT

The severity of punishment for rape depended on several factors: whether the victim was a virgin, where the rape occurred, the amount of resistance on the part of the woman and the social status of the victim or offender. Sadly, these same variables still determine the prosecution and possible conviction of the modern-day rapist.

A detailed description of Biblical law's penalty regarding the rape of a woman engaged to be married is in Deuteronomy: 23–27.

"If within the city a man comes upon a maiden

who is betrothed, and has relations with her, you shall bring them both out to the gate of the city and there stone them to death: the girl because she did not cry out for help though she was in the city, and the man because he violated his neighbor's wife. Thus you shall purge the evil from your midst."

Obviously if a woman was raped within the city limits she wouldn't report it for fear of death, since the law thought it impossible to be raped in a crowded area. The woman was punished because presumably she neglected to fight off her attacker and therefore she must have wanted to be raped. On the other hand, the man was punished for violating *his neighbor's wife* and not for raping the woman. He was stoned to death for committing a crime against a man.

"If however, it is in the open fields that a man comes upon such a betrothed maiden, seizes her and has relations with her, the man alone shall die. You shall do nothing to the maiden, since she is not guilty of a capital offense . . . it was in the open fields that he came upon her, and though the betrothed maiden may have cried out for help, there was no one there to come to her aid."

In this instance, the raped woman was spared the legal consequences. The law applied to the geography of the crime, not to the crime itself. She was just a possession which was moved to another area. There was no consideration for her human rights or emotions; she hadn't any.

Our present-day jurisprudence has stopped stoning rapists and their victims, but sometimes women victimized by rape continue to be punished through the treatment they receive from the police, medical personnel and courts. Only in a rape case is the victim sometimes required to first prove herself innocent before the rest of society will even begin to infer that her rapist is guilty.

Early English law, from which most of our legal precepts are taken, set different standards for the punishment and compensation for rape. Justice was administered on the basis of social position, varying with the rank of the rapist and his victim. For example, a man "who lay with a maiden belonging (not married) to the King" had to pay 50 shillings for the rape, but if she was a "grinding slave" the amount was cut in half. If a man raped a "nobleman's serving maid" he was fined 12 shillings; a "commoner's serving maid" netted no more than five shillings. However, if a slave raped a commoner's serving maid, he was castrated and if he dared to rape anyone above that rank, he was killed.

English law saw rape as a punishable crime, but the punishment depended on the importance of the victim. Unlike the Assyrian rape of retribution, the law condemned taking a pound of flesh, and instead, put a price tag on it by in effect ruling how much each pound of flesh was worth.

The law was as arbitrary to upper class rapists as it was to the victim. It was literally impossible for a king or bishop to rape anyone. One word said in their own behalf would automatically clear them of all charges. If a priest was accused of rape or any other misdeed, he could take an oath while wearing his vestments and swear before an altar that the charges were untrue. He would then be cleared of all wrongdoing.

Our rape laws have changed drastically since Tudor times but the bulk of the change has affected the rapist, not the victim. The law holds a man's past offenses as a sacred trust. He may have been arrested for and convicted of rape innumerable times. However, this information is sacrosanct and may not be mentioned in a courtroom. On the other hand, most states today allow a woman to be questioned about her personal sex life. Even though she is the one bringing criminal charges against a man, it seems sometimes that, during the trial, she herself is being judged. She can be held accountable and frequently judged on the basis of her chastity or the lack of it.

For many women who have been raped, justice has been more than blind. It has been biased against women. Moreover, modern law suffers from the remnants of this prejudice. Throughout history, it has been written and managed by men and so men's vision of justice often has left women at a painful disadvantage.

2
Myths
of Rape

In 1971, Dr. Menachim Amir, an Israeli criminologist, published *Patterns in Forcible Rape,* a book which shattered many of the prevailing myths about rape. Amir conducted an intensive survey of 646 rape cases handled by the Philadelphia Police Department from January to December of 1958 and January to December of 1960. This is the first book of its kind which deals with every aspect of forcible rape. The findings of Amir's study are seen frequently in this book.

MYTH   The primary motive for rape is sexual.

FACT   Studies show the major motive of rape is aggression, not sex. The rapist is seen to have a normal personality but an abnormal tendency to be aggressive and violent. Amir says it is this violence "which makes him (the rapist) a danger to the community."

MYTH   Rape is an impulse act.

FACT   Amir found that 71% of all rapes were planned; the rapist has it in his mind to rape a woman (any woman) or he has a specific woman in mind. Eleven per cent of rapes were partially planned.

13

For example, a rapist takes advantage of a woman in a situation where she is particularly vulnerable (when she was hitchhiking, walking alone at night, drunk, etc.) and only 16% were spontaneous or "explosive" rapes where the rapist had no prior intent to commit rape.

As a further breakdown, 90% of all gang rapes, 83% of pair rapes and 58% of all single rapes were planned.

MYTH Rape occurs only among strangers.
FACT Though 66% of the rapes studied by Amir did occur among strangers, a full 34% involved cases where the victim and offender know each other in some way. This familiarity runs the gamut from a casual acquaintanceship from living in the same vicinity or working at the same job to the closeness of a neighbor relationship between victim and rapist. In 14% of the cases the rapist is a close personal friend, a member of her family or friend of the family.

When considering these statistics, it's important to remember that Amir dealt with *reported* cases of forcible rape and a woman is more apt to report being raped by a stranger than to press charges against a friend or relative.

MYTH   No healthy woman can be raped because she is able to prevent it.

FACT   Ironically, this myth is perpetuated by the same people who are supposed to help rape victims. Some doctors, policemen and attorneys use this myth as a criterion for judging rape victims. However, the facts are different.

Amir found that in the majority of rapes the woman is threatened with death if she resists. In 87% of all rapes the rapist either carries a weapon or threatens her with death. Roughness occurs in 29% of the crimes, non-brutal beatings in 25%, brutal beatings in 20%, and choking in 12% of all rapes. No force whatsoever exists in only 15% of all rape cases studied by Amir and these instances usually involved the rape of a child.

MYTH   Women who are raped are asking for it.

FACT   Rape is a brutal, degrading, violent crime. Amir's studies show that most rapes are planned and the victim is usually threatened with death or bodily harm if she resists. Why would a woman go out of her way to be humiliated, to be beaten or possibly killed? The problem with this myth is the way it takes the criminal blame away from the rapist and shifts the responsibility for the crime to the victim.

Does a woman's dress or mannerisms give any man the right to rape her? Because you carry money in your pocket, does it mean that you're asking to be robbed? Perhaps this myth arose because rape is the only violent crime in which women are never the perpetrators, but always the victims.

MYTH   It can't happen to me.

FACT   I hope it will never happen to you but any woman, regardless of age, race or social status, can be and is raped. Reported rapes have occurred to females from six months to 93 years old. Amir found the ages of most rape victims in Philadelphia to be between 10–19, while the national average is 24 years old.

3
Who Are
the Rapists?

Our conception of the rapist is often as incorrect and garbled as our conceptions of his victim. In reality there is no typical rapist just as there is no typical victim. You can't pick them out in a crowd. He looks like other men and, in many ways except one, he *is* like other men.

There are no deciding physical attributes which set him apart. He isn't taller, burlier or more sinister than his brothers. He hasn't any superficial quality you can perceive. No early warning signal goes off in your mind to alarm you of the presence of a rapist. There are no visible clues.

The rapists studied by Amir were generally found to have normal sexual personalities, differing from the well-adjusted male in only one regard. Amir's rapists exhibited an often overwhelming tendency toward expressing violence and rage. This supports the fact that rape is not a sexual crime per se, but rather is a violent, aggressive act. Amir says, "Studies indicated that sex offenders do not constitute a unique or psychopathological type; nor are they as a group invariably more disturbed than the control groups to which they are compared."

A disconcerting fact is that rapists appear to be

"normal," normal in this sense meaning no different in appearance from society's accepted norm. Since he obviously doesn't wear a sign that he is a rapist, what protection do you have when your adversary can't be distinguished from an innocuous friend, acquaintance or stranger? The similarity between the rapist and other men complicates the problem of rape for women.

The Institute for Sex Research in Indiana, founded by Alfred Kinsey, analyzed convicted sex offenders in the late '40s and '50s and arrived at similar conclusions. "There are no outstandingly ominous signs in their (the rapists') presex-offense histories; indeed, their heterosexual adjustment is quantitatively well above average." The Institute carried Amir's findings one step further. Not only were rapists like other men, they were seemingly better adjusted. Instead of drawing a line to separate rapists from nonrapists, these studies broadened the possibilities. Does this mean all men are potential rapists?

A New York psychologist put it this way. "By virtue of their sex, you could say that all men are potential rapists, but that's a blanket statement. It's normal for men to think and fantasize about rape, but for the normal man, rape stays a fantasy. It's apparent the rapist isn't satisfied with the fantasy."

Perhaps there are no marked physical attributes among rapists, but why do they rape? What makes a young man attack a woman old enough to be his mother? Why do some rapists use brutal force in addition to sexually humiliating their victims? What would possess a man to rape a child?

There are studies and theories, studies of studies and theories about theories, but there is no one answer.

Dr. Amir found the largest age group among rapists to be 15–19 years old, followed by men 20–25 years of age. He also found that the older the rapist, the younger the victim. The Institute for Sex Research estimates the average rapist is 24½. According to Amir, rapists were generally unmarried and were at the lower end of the economic scale, from skilled laborer to unemployed. 25–33% of all Amir's rapists were married; the Institute says 33%. Amir also found that rapes occurred at specific times. 53% of all rapes took place on the weekends, with Saturday being the peak day, and almost half were committed between 8:00 P.M. and 2:00 A.M.

Half of all rapists studied by Amir had previous arrest records. Nine per cent were convicted of rape in the past and 4% were arrested for a sexual offense other than rape (exhibitionism, fetishism, etc.).

Concerning rape which occurs between blacks and whites, Amir reported that the majority of all rapes were intraracial (of the same race). Seventy-seven percent of black rapists raped black women, while 18% of white offenders raped white women. Amir's study contradicts the myth that rape is generally an interracial (of different races) crime.

In their attempt to identify the reasons for rape, psychologists, law-enforcement personnel and a score of other individuals have questioned and probed, trying to get inside the rapist's head to find out what makes him tick. We have theories, categories, cubby-holes and labels. However, there are no concrete conclusions.

The serious study of the psychological ingredients of a rapist is a relatively new undertaking. The first set of theories is only about four decades old and, as with any venture into the unknown, these studies are bound to make mistakes. Since there is no precedent to follow, the observations have a tendency to be general, to stereotype. On the other hand, some studies have established stringent guidelines as to the specific types of rapists. Though no one study is conclusive, all are in some way beneficial. It's a start in the right direction. People are beginning to concern themselves more with the "why" of rape rather than solely with the punishment for rape. In the past several years, the government has appropriated funds for the study of the rapist to get to the root of his problem before he commits a crime.

Some prevailing theories about the internal workings of a rapist are presented below. A few may strike you as being oversimplistic, others may appear confining. They may not be conclusive, but for the moment they are all we have.

THE CRIMINAL vs. THE PSYCHIATRIC RAPIST

Dr. Amir divided rapists into two broad categories which he labeled "criminal" and "psychiatric." According to Amir, the criminal rapist usually had a past criminal record of offenses like exhibitionism, fetishism, etc. His record most often began while he was an adolescent and he probably has raped before. This does not necessarily mean that he was ever convicted for rape or that he ever will be convicted.

As part of his personality profile, the criminal rapist was seen by Amir to be generally antisocial, easily influenced by his surroundings and peers and had very few inner restraints. His sexual urge was one of those he could not restrain. Amir found that the criminal rapist generally came from a lower class background, had little formal education and was often black.

Before you discount Dr. Amir's judgment about rapists because he classified most of them as black, remember that Amir studied only those rapes which were committed in the city of Philadelphia. He was viewing a predominantly urban situation where blacks comprised the majority of both rapists *and* victims. This is not to say that blacks rape more than whites, which is completely untrue. However, what it does say is that Amir dealt with the crime in a city where blacks outnumbered whites in the population.

Therefore, Amir based his assumptions on the percentages of what he saw. The geographic density and location of the offenders and victims were the deciding factors in his observations. Race, education or social status were not.

Based on the locale of his subjects, Amir saw the psychiatric rapist as generally well educated, with a higher than average IQ, and often coming from a higher economic bracket. He was thought to rape because of some personal inadequacy and he may have felt guilty after the rape. He was often a white man.

I want to stress that Amir arrived at these conclusions because of the location of his sample. These conclusions are not true for rape viewed on a national scale. They are correct only in terms of the crime as studied solely in the city of Philadelphia at the time of the study.

THE BRIDGEWATER STUDY

The Center for Diagnosis and Treatment of Sexually Dangerous Persons, in Bridgewater, Mass., conducted a study of more than 100 men convicted of rape and acknowledges three types of rapists.

Their first category of rapists are primarily motivated by aggressive feelings toward women in general. In an interview with *Newsweek* magazine, August 20, 1973, psychologist Ralph Garofalo, who conducted the Bridgewater Study, stated that "Their (the rapists') sexual behavior is in the service of aggression, serving to humiliate, dirty and defile the victim." Their rage often leads to violence which results in the beating, mutilating or even murdering of the victim. This category of rapists has built up a rage from some personal experience in their childhood which has led them to hate and despise women. The Bridgewater Study feels that these men tend to place "Women" (particularly their mothers) on a kind of pedestal. However, the women with whom they come into contact on an everyday basis are untrustworthy, sly, officious and generally contemptible. In this case, the rapist's idealized view of women conflicts with what he sees them to be in reality. This feeling of being cheated creates the rage.

The Bridgewater Center's second group of rapists is comprised of men whose prime motivation is sex. These are men with a history of voyeurism, exhibitionism and fetishism and they have an innate, intense feeling of inadequacy. They live most of their lives fantasizing about being supervirile men but feel impotent and inadequate in a normal sexual relationship. The study claims these men are trying to suppress their homosexual feelings and bases this assumption on the Freudian "strong mother, weak father" syndrome. This would seem to be a convenient label to tag on a man who doesn't follow the norm. I believe the Center's reference to homosexuality is totally unfounded. By categorizing rapists as repressed homosexuals, the study implies that all such men with repressed homosexual tendencies are sick and capable of sexually-motivated rape.

The study continues its portrait of this group by stating that these men act out their fantasies by raping or attempting to rape women and are often clumsy, shy rapists. They are easily frightened by women who offer resistance.

One such rapist, jailed in Canada on a rape charge and who had previous offenses of voyeurism, exhibitionism and indecent assault, said in an interview with a prison psychologist: "I'm at it eight hours or it might be three, then it might be twelve . . . Well, I don't have to be dangerous to be a sex offender because most of my activities are not dangerous at all. I'm walking up and down the street and I'm sitting on a bus trying to peer at girls' legs and stuff like that. Well, that's not dangerous, you know what I mean, but I'm active all the time. . . . Now when I picked up several girls I had the intention in mind of not raping them. I said to myself, well I'll pull out my penis and play with it and that and I'll make obscene remarks to her. This is what I say to myself and this is what I did. Now if I say to myself, I'm taking this girl up and I'm going to rape her I don't know whether I would or not."

Men in this category are rarely violent toward their victims and often attempt to rape women they have seen before and fantasized about.

One 16-year-old rapist, a small, fragile young man who was charged with six rapes, was described in *The New York Times* as always "contritely and sincerely" telling his victims that "he couldn't help himself" and would apologize after every rape.

Simply, these are men who dream the impossible dream. They are unable to have a normal sex life, so they resort to rape. By raping a woman, the man is no longer the same weak, submissive male who stares back at him every time he looks in the mirror.

Bridgewater's last and most dangerous group of all rapists is the psychopaths, men who rape because of an explosion of sex and aggression. These are the sadistic, brutal rapes which every one of us has read about in the papers. Garofalo believes that these men discharge anger best through a sadistic sexual act. They are explosive, angry men.

THE INSTITUTE FOR SEX RESEARCH STUDY

On the basis of detailed interrogations with convicted rapists, Kinsey's Institute for Sex Research arrived at five categories of offenders.

The first type is what the Institute called the "assaultive variety." Twenty-five to thirty-three per cent of rapists questioned were in this group.

These rapists use unnecessary violence and strong threats when they rape. They are sadistic men who are often compelled to punish and hurt the victim. The assaultive rapist gets his kicks through the use of force, not from the sexual intercourse. The women are generally strangers and the rapists may carry a weapon of some kind. Brandishing a gun or knife adds to their feelings of "machismo," the self-image of a dominant, aggressive, brutal male.

The assaultive rapist hates women, all women, and typically steals something, no matter how trivial, from the victim after the rape. A 63-year-old California woman, raped at gunpoint by a 24-year-old man, was robbed of $2 after the rape. His parting words were "I bet I made your day." He then threw her a kiss and ran away.

According to the Institute, these men delude themselves into believing that they are actually wanted and desired by their victims and "they seem to find it difficult to believe that the women bear them any ill will."

2. Twelve to twenty-six per cent of rapists interviewed are described as "amoral delinquents." These men aren't sadistic and they don't hate women. It's just that they don't think too much of them. This type of rapist is looking for any woman, and as far as they're concerned, women are nothing more than sexual objects placed on earth to fulfill their needs. This man is entirely egocentric. The world revolves around him. If he wants something, he takes it.

3. Thirty-nine per cent are termed the "drunken variety," since they were found to be drunk at the time of the rape. Both Amir and the Institute feel that alcohol affects the man's tendency toward ag-

gression by lowering his sober, natural restraints to the point where he would presume to rape a woman or hazily misconstrue her efforts to resist. In some instances, alcohol literally turns a man into a violent maniac, ultimately resulting in a brutal, sadistic rape.

4. Almost ten per cent of rapes are called "explosive." For some unknown reason, a man who has led a seemingly normal life suddenly rapes a woman. Something snaps in his mind. The rape is spontaneous and may or may not be brutal. The causes of this explosion would seem to vary with the man. These rapes are unpredictable and inexplicable. The rapist can be anyone from a criminal, a high school student to the man next door.

5. Another ten per cent fall into the "double-standard variety." The Institute states that these men divide women into "good" women, whom they treat with respect, and "bad" women, who are "not entitled to consideration if they become obstinate." Men in this category are chivalrous to women they feel are moral and upstanding. They would never dream of raping one. On the other hand, their subjective idea of bad women leads them to think these women are sexually promiscuous and, therefore, open to rape. The Institute quoted one rapist's rationalization as "Man, these dumb broads don't know what they want. They get you worked up and then they try to chicken out. You let 'em get away with stuff like that and

the next thing you know they'll be walking all over you."

The thoughts and reflections of rape victims follow painfully similar lines. Their stories unite around pain, helplessness and the horror of the act itself. Rape is the invasion of public criminality into a woman's most private world. But women also react with anger and bitterness to the aftermath of a rape. Hospitals, police, the courts, even friends and lovers help little, and sometimes injure, by their reactions.

"The most disgusting thing was that I felt like a piece of meat; not a person. It was as though I didn't have feelings anymore—it didn't matter who I was or how I felt.

"I was just about to get into my car, when a man came up from behind me. He grabbed me around the neck and he had a knife in his hand. He said if I screamed, he would carve today's date on my chest. I didn't scream and never told anyone about it until weeks later . . . It was almost as if it had never happened to me. I couldn't admit it to myself, let alone to anyone else.

"I finally told the man who I'd been dating for several years, and when I came to the part where the rapist said he'd carve the date on my chest, Bob stopped looking into my eyes and looked down at my chest. For a split second, he grinned—my God, he actually grinned.

". . . That was all it took to make me realize that rape wasn't a man's problem at all. He

*couldn't be raped, so he couldn't understand.
Here with a man I really cared for, who had more
empathy for the rapist than for me."*

This is the story of a 28-year-old nurse who
was raped as she walked to her car in a hospital
parking lot. The faces, ages and circumstances of
rape victims are different, but the pain is the
same. A woman who has been forcibly raped has
her own personal horror story; a hidden, rarely
considered fear has become reality.

A PRIVATE CRIME, A SOCIAL HORROR

Rape—the most commonly committed violent
crime—the least reported and the least often punished.

According to the *Uniform Crime Reports* published by the FBI, 67,131 women were raped in
1978. This is a 6.5% rise over 1977. However,
the figures are deceiving. It's estimated that for
every rape reported to the police, ten are not,
bringing the total estimated rapes to a staggering
738,441 in 1978.

The three major categories of violent crime
listed by the FBI are forcible rape, murder and
aggravated assault. (An aggravated assault is an
attack, with or without a deadly weapon, which
results in injury and also includes any attempted
assault with a deadly weapon.) In comparing the
per cent change of violent crime in the U.S. from

1977 to 1978, murder rose by 2.3% and aggravated assault increased by 6.8%, while *reported* rapes rose by 6.5%. Even with the increased frequency of the crime and more women reporting it, rape still has the lowest conviction rate of any violent crime. In one recent year, only 133 out of every 1,000 men tried for rape actually received convictions.

Rape is not an isolated crime. Every time a woman is raped, all women are affected. It makes us more fearful and confused. We are afraid for ourselves, our daughters, sisters and friends.

4
Dangerous Places

The Streets

Do not go gentle into that good night
—Dylan Thomas

More than one-half of all rapes committed in the United States either begin or end in the streets. The rapist frequently finds a woman walking the streets, rapes her there or pulls her into his car and drives to another place. The streets are the place where the rapist most often finds his quarry.

Your probability of being raped increases once the sun goes down. Darkness affords a blanket of protection for the would-be rapist, shielding him—in the dimness of an alley or storefront, behind trees, bushes or in the blackness of a poorly lit parking lot. The fear of being raped forces many women to relinquish their right to walk the streets at night. You should never take a night walk alone, even though it seems ridiculous and unfair to be condemned to spending the rest of your unescorted evenings sealed behind a locked door.

Because of their jobs, some women must walk at night to get to their cars or to wait for public transportation. They are particularly prone to attack. If you work at night, ask a fellow employee if she is going in the same direction and walk with her. Rapists choose the most vulnerable vic-

35

tims and are discouraged by more than one woman. Make an indelible mark in your mind that rapists prefer easy prey and there is tremendous strength in numbers. If you have a car, why not ask if you can drop another woman off at the bus stop, subway or train station if it's on your way home. When you help another woman, you're also helping yourself.

Whenever you walk the streets, stay close to the curb. Rapists have been known to wait in alleys, doorways and storefronts and to literally snatch victims as they walk past. The most important thing about walking alone is to walk briskly and confidently. You must give the impression that you know where you're going, with no hesitation or worry of getting there. Don't look as though you're lost, or as if your mind is a million miles away. This is precisely what the rapist wants. Don't look vulnerable, look aggressive and strong.

Don't overburden yourself by carrying a multitude of packages or books. If you begin to accumulate a number of packages while shopping, have the store send them to your home. You don't want to appear like a pack animal with both arms wrapped around a stack of bundles. Keep your hands free.

The same applies to your pocketbook. Put your purse on a bathroom scale to see how much it weighs. This may seem like an odd idea, but the fact is, many women lug up to fourteen pounds of paraphernalia in their pocketbooks. If your purse tips the scales at a walloping ten to fourteen pounds, think seriously about separating the wheat from the chaff. You are not outfitting yourself for an Arctic expedition, so only carry what's necessary.

Your clothing is a good indicator of your chances for fleeing from an attacker. Attempting to run in platform shoes or clogs is like trying to skip while wearing stilts. It just can't be done. Wear non-confining clothes and shoes.

When you walk, choose well-lighted streets and avoid streets where there are a lot of bars. If you find yourself on a dark, deserted road, don't walk on the pavement. Walk in the middle of the street and get off of it as soon as you reach the end of the block.

EXCUSE ME, MISS?

Whatever you do, never stop to give a man directions at night. If he asks you for a match or wants to start a conversation, don't say anything, keep walking. One woman was stopped by a man who wanted directions to the nearest police station and asked if she would please write them down, since he was a stranger in town. As she reached into her pocketbook for a pencil, he pulled her into an alley and raped her.

These are not simplistic warnings. They are mentioned because women who were in these same situations were raped. It is admirable to be a Good Samaritan, but it's imperative to think of your safety first.

Say you are walking down the street and a car

pulls along side of you. This is a common ploy used to pull women into cars. Turn around immediately, walk behind the car and cross quickly to the other side of the street. The same applies if you notice a parked car on the side of the road with the motor running. Cross the street and leave the area as fast as you can.

If you are walking and get the feeling that you are being followed, turn around and look. If you're the least bit suspicious of the person behind you, cross the street and walk in the opposite direction. Head towards the nearest lighted building and tell the person inside that you are being followed. Call the police and don't leave the building until help arrives.

If you are being followed in a residential area, run to the nearest lighted house and bang on the door with every ounce of energy you have. This isn't a social visit, so don't knock politely on the door. Yell "FIRE," not "Rape," or "Help." If you scream "Rape!," statistics prove that people within hearing range will run, but not in your direction. Sadly, people find it easier to react to natural disasters than to come to the aid of other human beings. Yelling "Fire!" produces a kind of no-fault humanitarian reaction by which a person can help in an innocuous way without taking on the responsibility of being involved.

In 1973, a 20-year-old New Jersey woman was raped in broad daylight on a sidewalk near Trenton, in full view of 24 male employees of a nearby roofing company. According to the *New*

York Times, the men "watched intently" but did not answer her screams for help. One of the men who stood by said, "We all feel bad about it now . . . but we really thought it was just a couple of nuts, and it made a good show at the time."

In another incident in July of 1974, an off-duty New York City policeman was walking the street when he saw three men carrying a woman into an apartment. The officer followed the men up several flights of stairs, identified himself and pulled out his service revolver as the would-be rapists were in the process of undressing the unconscious woman. For 40 minutes the policeman held the rapists at bay while yelling and knocking on the apartment doors for help. No one responded. "I knocked on five doors," the officer later said, "and nobody would make that lousy call to help me." Finally, the policeman ordered the men outside and fired two shots into the air. At last, someone dialed the police emergency number and a squad car arrived because "a man with a gun" was reported to be in the area.

Driving Your Car

You are somewhat safer in the privacy of your car, but not much. Wherever there's a will to rape, there's a way to find a victim.

Check the back seat and floor of your car before getting in. Rapists often crouch behind the seat and pounce on the unsuspecting woman when she gets into her car. Always lock the car doors and avoid parking on deserted streets and parking lots. When you go to the supermarket or shopping center, park as close as you can to the store, particularly at night. Be sure to have the keys ready in your hands, so you won't have to fumble for them in the parking lot. Don't loiter around your car, get into it as soon as you can.

If a man approaches the car when you're stopped at a traffic light, look both ways, keep your hand on the horn and step on the gas. Don't wait for the light to turn green. If you want to keep a window open, roll down the one that is nearest to you, not the window opposite you.

Put your pocketbook and any packages you might have on the floor or in the glove compartment, not on the front seat. Bundles like those, easily visible, are open invitations for passers-by who might be toying with the idea of entering your car.

If you think a car is following you, keep your hand on the horn and head toward the nearest police station or business district. Don't go home; he'll follow you. If it's possible, make a mental note of the model and color of his car and remember it. If you have the opportunity to get a look at the license plate, write it down and give it to the police. The most important thing is to get away from the car, so don't go out of your way to try and see the license number. Sometimes, the car behind you will flash its headlights off and on. Don't pull over. Ignore it and continue driving. Many women, mistakenly believing the flashing headlights belonged to a police car, pulled to the side of the road to find the bogus policeman was actually a rapist. If the car behind you is really a police car, there will be flashing blue or red lights from the top of the car and a loud siren. Disregard everything else.

Anytime you get into the car, make sure there is at least one-quarter of a tank of gas. If you must stop for gas at night, stay in the car and if you have to use the telephone, lock your purse in the glove compartment, take the keys and just enough money to make the call.

KEYS

Ideally, house keys should be separated from car keys. If you do keep them on the same chain, be sure to remove the house and trunk key when you park your car in a private lot. Parking lot attendants have been known to copy house keys while you're away and trace your address from the license plate number.

If you carry the kind of key chain that has space for the name and address of the owner, throw it away; it's dangerous. It's better to lose your keys than to have a stranger know where you live and, what's worse, have the key to get into your home.

You'll have to exert the same amount of caution when pulling into your driveway. Put on the high beams and leave them on until you open the garage door. Once you lock the garage, keep the house key ready in your hand.

CAR TROUBLE

You're driving alone on the expressway, freeway or turnpike and suddenly your car breaks down. Pull over to the side of the road, keep your doors locked and windows up and stay in the car. Police recommend raising the hood of the car as a signal for help, but before you get out of that car, look around and make sure no one is around. Turnpikes, expressways, freeways and major roads are patrolled by police, so you'll receive help eventually.

If a man stops to help you, keep the windows up—or open to a crack—and ask him to stop at the nearest phone and call for assistance. Don't get out of the car or let him try to fix it. Not every man who stops to help you is a rapist, but there is no way for you to tell. He may have the best intentions, but anytime you are in a potentially susceptible situation you have to be wary.

HIGHWAY FLARES

Road flares should be kept in the glove compartment of your car in the event of car trouble at night. The 12-inch paper-covered flare is shaped like a candle. It's easy to use and doesn't require a match. Pulling the clothlike tab on the side of the flare exposes a matchlike top which can be scratched against any hard surface. When you scrape the top against the ground, the flare ignites, but scrape it away from your body, making sure the wind is at your back.

Most flares have a metal stake at one end so you can punch it into the ground behind your car. Road flares give off a brilliant red light which can be seen at great distances. They can be purchased at most hardware and auto supply stores in two sizes, 15 or 30 minute flares; they cost about 40 cents.

TO STOP OR NOT TO STOP

If you're driving along the highway and spot a disabled car on the side of the road, your first thought may be to stop and offer assistance. This is an admirable thought, but don't. You'll be more helpful by noting the location of the car and then stopping at the first safe telephone and calling the police or highway patrol. Dial the operator and she or he will connect you with the police.

One rapist's modus operandi was to stop his car on the roadside, raise the hood and flag down passing motorists. If a man answered his call for help, he would simply say that he was waiting for the police; but when a woman stopped, it was another story. The man admitted to successfully raping 11 women by forcing them into his car and then driving to an isolated area.

Public Transportation

The cavernous pits of subways are dangerous at any hour of the day. The tunnels give you little freedom to run and very few places to run safely to. If you use the subway, carry a freon horn in your hand (the horn is described in the chapter on self-defense) and not in your pocketbook. The horn is extremely effective in scaring off an attacker. It lets off a shrill blast which bounces off the walls, making it much louder.

While you wait for the train to arrive, stand next to the change booth and don't go near the edge of the platform. Once on the train, avoid sitting near groups of men or in deserted cars. Stay alert, this is no place for a nap. If you are bothered by a man on the subway, don't get off at your normal stop unless it's well lit and populated. Ride further until you come to a busy subway stop and then get off. If he follows you, go directly to the change booth and tell the attendant. She or he will call the police.

Buses—Waiting for a bus at night is a risky proposition. Avoid waiting on isolated street corners, walk to a stop near a business district which is well lit and populated. Stand away from the curb until the bus arrives and once on the bus, sit near the driver. If anyone bothers you, tell the driver and he or she will drop you off at a safe place.

Hitchhiking

Never—no matter how pitiful, young or helpless a male hitchhiker appears—Never pick him up. Even if there is someone else in your car. Countless numbers of women are raped by hitchhikers. Whatever you do, don't let a stranger into your back seat. You'll be vulnerable to attack.

Women should never hitchhike; it's the most dangerous means of transportation. If, however, you do spot a woman thumbing a ride, it'll be your decision. Women, of course, are not, simply because of their sex, safe passengers. On the other hand, by picking her up, you may have saved her from being raped. Think over the risks *first*.

Baby-Sitting

Baby-sitting for strangers can be a potentially hazardous way to earn a few dollars unless you take the proper precautions to ensure that the people for whom you are sitting are really in need of a baby sitter. You can't afford to take the word of a stranger in good faith.

In June of 1974, a 14-year-old Maryland girl placed an ad in a local paper, offering her services as a baby sitter. The man who answered the ad said he needed a sitter and told her to take a bus to the stop nearest his house, where his wife would meet her. The trusting teenager followed his directions and hasn't been heard from since.

The stranger's phone number turned out to be the number of a nearby phone booth.

· This is only one example of the tragic outcomes of women who have accepted jobs from strangers without knowing if it was a legitimate situation.

TIPS FOR BABY SITTERS

1. Whenever a stranger answers your advertisement or calls you to sit, take the name, address and telephone number. If you should decide to accept the job, call the number several hours later (don't mention that you're going to call). Identify yourself and ask about some 'forgotten' information like the age of the child, the time to put the child to bed or if you should bring your own dinner. This is important to ensure the number isn't a hoax and does actually belong to the person who first contacted you.

2. If you are asked to baby-sit by people in the neighborhood but haven't sat for them before, ask your friends if they know these people and find out if they are nice people to work for.

3. Anytime you baby-sit, write down the name, address and phone number of the people, the time you are expected to stop sitting and leave this information with your parents or with a friend. Call home when you arrive at the house and ask your parents to call you near the time you are expected to leave, just to make sure that everything is all right.

4. Sometimes the people will offer to pick you up and bring you to their house. If they are strangers, don't accept the offer. Instead, have a member of your family or a friend take you. Don't let them just drop you off in front of the house, have them come inside and meet the people. If you feel uncomfortable or uneasy with them, don't hesitate to tell them that you would rather not sit.

5. Once inside the house, lock all the doors and turn at least one light on in every room.

6. Before the people leave, ask if they are expecting any calls and write down the names of the people. If anyone else calls, ask who it is and never tell them the exact time you expect the people to return or how long you have been sitting.

7. If you hear any strange noises outside, or if a stranger keeps calling on the phone, call the police immediately, then call your parents. Don't leave the house.

5
How
to Avoid
Rape

Securing Your Home or Apartment

More than one-third of all rapes occur in the home, so it's imperative that you take some necessary precautions to lessen your vulnerability to ever being raped. The first place to begin rape-proofing your home or apartment is the front door. Push, rap, bang, shake and poke your door to see if it rattles. If you find that your door offers little resistance, think what easy prey a rapist or burglar will find it. A cheap, plywood door fastened by weak hinges affords no more protection than a moist piece of cardboard. Most amateur burglars and professional rapists won't take the time to pick a lock if they can enter your home by applying a small amount of brute force to the front door. If your door is wobbly, it's probably because the hinges are either worn or loose. Take a screwdriver and tighten the bolts that hold the hinges to the door. If there's still no improvement, it may be that the door is too small for the frame. Replace the door.

The builders of apartments and new homes are notorious for cutting down costs by installing cheap, poor-quality door frames and locks, so you should seriously consider adding another lock to your door.

KEY-IN-THE-KNOB LOCK

The most commonly installed lock in apartment houses is the key-in-the-knob or spring latch lock. It works by inserting a key into the doorknob and has a button on the inside of the door which you press in to lock the door when you're home. This is the loser of all front door locks. It can be opened easily by a subtle attack on the door (jimmying) or by inserting a credit card, college ID card or any slim, hard object between the latch (the metal piece which protrudes from the lock) and the door jamb (the metal plate on the door frame opposite the door).

If you have this type of lock, look to see if it has a small bolt (trigger bolt) protruding from the latch. If your lock has a trigger bolt, you're somewhat better off, but not much. Since the average trigger bolt only goes one-quarter to one-eighth of an inch into the door jamb, this lock is easy pickings for anyone who wants to get in, including yourself if you don't have your key.

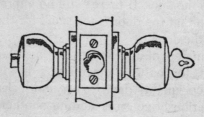

Key-in-the-knob Lock

VERTICAL-BOLT LOCK

The most inexpensive way to convert the key-in-the-knob lock into a good one is to buy a vertical-bolt or dead-bolt lock and add it to your door. You can purchase one at your local hardware store for about $18 and it's well worth the investment.

The beauty of the dead-bolt lock is that it's virtually jimmyproof. An intruder would have to chop down the door to get in. This lock has a solid metal bar which slides into a plate made of case-hardened steel rings that is fastened to the other side of the door plate.

Make sure you buy a dead-bolt lock that has a vertical metal bar at least one inch long. If you

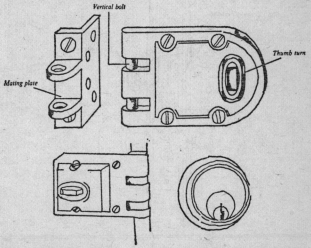

Vertical bolt

Thumb turn

Mating plate

Vertical-bolt Lock

opt to install it yourself, use long wood screws that have a deep grooved pattern necessary for gripping into your door. Measure the thickness of the door before deciding to use the screws that come with the lock. Be sure they are long enough to burrow well into the door frame.

MORTISE LOCK

If you already have a mortise lock on your front door, consider yourself lucky, since they are rarely installed in apartment buildings. Mortise locks have the convenience of the key-in-the-knob lock with the added security of the dead bolt. This lock works in two ways: by inserting a key from

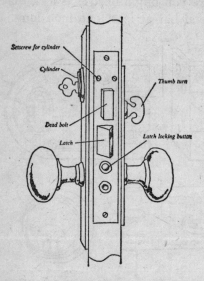

Mortise Lock

the outside of the door and by turning the thumb-turn on the inside. You can set the thumb-turn so it will lock from the inside when you turn the knob. As an added security, the rectangular dead bolt extends about one-half to one inch into the door jamb and can't be opened with a credit card the way a key-in-the-knob lock can.

PEEPHOLES

The peephole or through-the-door viewing device is a must for apartment dwellers. It is shaped like a small telescope with a piece of glass at either end and a wide-angle lens inside, much like the lens on a camera. This device gives you the security of looking outside without the person seeing you.

Peepholes come in various sizes and shapes. However, the one recommended by most locksmiths is the kind which requires drilling a small hole about a half-inch in diameter or less into the door. It costs about $5 for a peephole and installation—less if you do it yourself.

Let's assume your door is fortified properly, locks are secure, door frame is steady and peephole is in place. Still, there is one more problem. Someone rings the doorbell, you look through the peephole and find it's a stranger. No amount of psychological intuition can instantly tell you who this person really is. Since rapists frequently pose as salesmen, utilitymen and policemen, it's unwise to open your door to anyone without checking identification. This is where the chain lock is important.

CHAIN LOCKS

The chain lock is used frequently by apartment dwellers. It serves as a checkpoint Charlie of sorts. The lock is mounted on the inner surface of the door, permitted it to open about three to four inches, depending on the length of the chain. You can buy a sturdy chain lock for about $6, but make sure the chain is a thick, heavy metal that is short enough to prevent an arm from reaching in and unlocking the chain. You want an opening only large enough to pass an identification card through it.

When you install this lock, use long screws (some chain locks come with very short screws, making it a simple process to snap the chain from its base). Attach the chain slide (the long rectangular piece connected to the chain) on a slant. Don't mount it straight across. A straight mount-

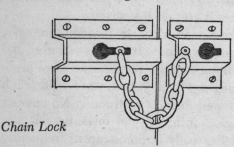

Chain Lock

ing makes it easier to unlatch the chain from the outside.

This lock is useless if you use it alone, since the chain can be broken by a hard elbow to the door. The purpose of the chain lock is to check the credentials of strange men who for some reason want to get into your home.

WHICHEVER LOCK YOU CHOOSE ...

Even the finest hardware on your front door is worthless unless you remember to keep your door locked *at all times*. Anytime you leave the house, whether for a short sprint to the laundry room or to pick up your mail, always lock your door.

LOCKSMITHS vs. DO-IT-YOURSELF

You can install any of the locks mentioned in this book. However, the do-it-yourself method can pose some problems for the novice, particularly with front door locks. The locksmith is the best person to advise you of the most reliable lock for your needs and it's his business to sell and install high-quality locks.

The drawback of hiring a locksmith is the expense. Their fees vary, but generally are determined by the amount of time spent away from the shop. To cut down on costs, make a list of things to ask the locksmith before you go to his shop: the type of lock you presently have on the door, the kind of protection you want (dead bolt, chain, window, sliding door locks, etc.), and the physical characteristics of the door itself. Talk to him in the shop so he won't have to spend time in your apartment or home. Then set a date. You won't be charged for the initial consultation in the shop.

Another problem is the reliability of the locksmith. Anyone can put up a sign and declare that he or she is a locksmith. They aren't licensed, so before you hire this person, ask if he is a member of the National Locksmiths Association, which bonds its members, or the Associated Locksmiths of America, a self-regulating organization.

Answering the Door

Never let any stranger into your house without first checking his ID. Telephone repairmen, salesmen, poll takers, policemen—anyone whose business takes them into private homes is supposed to carry an identification card. Uniforms aren't enough. They can easily be stolen by a clever rapist before he begins his assaults.

If, for example, a man says he's from the gas company, ask to see his ID. He should have one. If he doesn't, or if you are suspicious for any reason (he might appear hesitant, might stutter, or might claim his company never issued IDs—false, they all do), ask for the name and telephone number of his immediate superior and make a phone call *before* you let him in. Even if he gives you no visible reasons to suspect him, be overly cautious anyway. Many men who rape, rape often. They will approach you calmly and sincerely; they've practiced. It's better to distrust and be slightly embarrassed when you are wrong about him than be right about him—and be raped.

One Midwestern rapist would rap on apartment house doors and tell the women who answered that he was from the sheriff's department. If she asked to see identification, he would show her his honorary ID from the police department. He was seldom further questioned with his fake ID; he successfully used this tactic for raping eight women.

Beware of any card that has "honorary" or "auxiliary member" on it. They are worthless and are often handed out in some cities as a fund-raising gimmick.

The same precautions must be used if a man identifies himself as a policeman. One quick flash of the badge before your eyes doesn't mean a thing. Look at the badge and read it carefully. It should have the officer's number and the name of the city on it. Watch out for badges which have "Sheriff of Gotham City" or "Captain—Royal Mounted Police." Remember that toy companies manufacture these tin insignias for children and they're often the size and shape of real police badges.

If someone comes to your door and asks to use your phone, leave him waiting outside and make the call for him. Never let a strange man into your apartment or home.

Furthermore, if the door bell rings at night when you aren't expecting anyone, say loudly "I'll get it Bill" (or any male name you prefer), and then answer the door. You don't want a stranger to know you're alone.

A WORD ABOUT CHILDREN

Children are extremely open and trusting toward strangers. Never let small children answer the door. Often they'll open it first, then run and get you. The same applies to children answering the telephone. If your child is old enough to understand, tell her or him not to give out any information over the phone: where you live, if the child is alone, if she or he has a daddy, if he is home or when he is expected back, etc.

SECURING WINDOWS

According to national crime reports, most illegal entries are made through doors, but windows follow a close second. If you live on the ground floor of an apartment building, your windows should be protected by a steel grate on the outside. This should have been installed by the builders. However, if your apartment lacks this security, your first plan of action is to gather the other tenants together and needle the superintendent to put them in. If you decide to install the metal grates yourself, it can cost anywhere from 60 to 120 dollars.

Other windows easily are protected by installing a simple window frame lock. This lock works with a key, is difficult to pick and costs only a few dollars.

Be sure to close the drapes or blinds at night. Rapists often wander, peeping first and choosing their victims beforehand. If it's obvious that you are alone, you're that much more vulnerable.

SLIDING DOORS

A sliding door is nothing more than a giant window which is easily removed by lifting it out of the frame. If the door track is on the inside, it can be fortified by placing a broomstick or metal rod in the channel on the floor. However, if the track is on the outside, it requires a lock. There are special locks for sliding doors which can be purchased at any hardware store. They resemble a dead bolt lock and cost a few dollars.

Lighting

Good lighting is a deterrent to any would-be rapist or burglar and is tremendously important to your safety. Take a look at your home or apartment in the same way you would if you were a prospective tenant. Be critical and be prepared to make some changes.

All parking areas should be well lit. If you have to hold your key in the air to see if it's the right one, your lighting is inadequate. All walkways, paths and steps should be brightly lit and any tall shrubbery close to paths should be trimmed.

Overgrown bushes are perfect camouflage for a waiting rapist.

Garages are another likely spot for unwanted visitors. Have at least one 100-watt bulb positioned on either side of the garage and be sure to close the garage door every time you leave the house. An open door is a standing invitation to a rapist, who knows the house is empty and may wait until you return.

The hallways and entrances to your apartment must be bathed in light. An individual is relatively limited in what she can do to improve apartment house lighting, but there is strength in numbers. If the tenants act as a group, they are often effective in pressuring landlords to install and maintain good lighting. Local building regulations are geared toward safe lighting, so if your landlord refuses to comply, contact your local building inspector and she or he will check your apartment.

Telephones

Never list your first name in the telephone book. You'll leave yourself wide open for crank calls and sick callers. Give your first initial and last name only, or, better yet (since it's now common knowledge that "S. Jones" is a female), give your first two initials, then your last name. When a man dials the wrong number, never give your name or phone number. Ask what number he is trying to call, tell him he misdialed and to try again.

At some point in almost every woman's life, she receives an obscene phone call. Remember, you aren't Dial-a-Prayer, so you don't have to be courteous. In fact, don't say anything. Just slam the phone down as hard as you can. This sudden jolt to his eardrums usually will discourage a sick caller from calling back. But, if he does call again, tell the phone company. And if he pesters you in the interim, tap once on the mouthpiece and say, "Yes, operator, please trace the call now." This trick worked for me several years ago.

Sometimes persons claiming to be poll takers call and ask you personal questions: are you married, do you live alone, where do you work, etc. Refuse to give out any personal information. The caller may be trying to set you up for a possible rape or burglary. Even if he isn't, it's none of his damned business. One woman was called by a man claiming to represent a dancing school. He said that she would be entitled to three free lessons if she could answer his questions correctly. One of the questions was if she lived alone. She made the mistake of answering him and was raped in her home the following evening.

Condition yourself to answer the phone with a healthy dash of paranoia. Keep in mind that convicted rapists have admitted to spending hours, even days, devising tricks to catch you off guard. Your best protection is training yourself to be in a constant state of caution.

For example, when it's necessary to give your phone number to strange agencies or persons you don't know well, give them your daytime office number if you work. Then be sure your fellow employees understand that they should never divulge any personal facts about you when they answer the phone.

Women Who Live in Apartments

Our apartment-oriented society poses a serious threat to women who live alone. Though surrounded by wall-to-wall people, apartment dwellers are often isolated from their neighbors, frequently by choice. We spend so much of our time in the company of others that we treasure any hours of privacy we can muster. But for safety's sake, it's essential to know your neighbors. You don't have to like them, just know them. Exchange telephone numbers and tell your neighbor you'll keep an eye on her apartment when she's away. Chances are, she'll do the same for you. Be extra wary of male neighbors you don't know well; a high percentage of rapes are committed by the man next door.

The second rule of apartment living is never put your first name or use Ms. or Miss on your mailbox. The Boston strangler and other lesser-known rapists found their victims by scanning female names on apartment house mailboxes. Use your first initial and last name only, or even better, just your last name.

Some superintendents ask for a key to your apartment to use in case of fire. This is a poor practice and from the standpoint of fire is totally ridiculous. The most common route of entry in case of fire is by breaking down the front door, not by wasting precious time trying to find the super and get your key. Furthermore, if the super's keys are stolen or copied, you're helpless. If you have a close friend in the apartment building, give her a copy of your key and tell the super she has it. If he still refuses, put the key into an envelope, seal it with wax and write your name on the wax before it dries. This will discourage the superintendent from entering your apartment when you are out. Check the envelope periodically, at least annually.

Never hide your house key under the doormat, in a flowerpot or over the door frame. A rapist or burglar knows just as many common hiding places as you, and more.

Laundry rooms and elevators are also territories frequented by rapists. The laundry room, often located in the basement, is an isolated, noisy cubicle which muffles your cries for help. When you do your laundry, get in and out of that room as quickly as possible and don't forget to lock your front door on the way out.

Elevators are small, soundproof boxes that can be stopped between floors indefinitely. Any time you get on an elevator, stand near the control panel and don't get on with a strange man. If the man makes a threatening move toward you, press the emergency button—not the stop button. This will set off an alarm which can be heard throughout the building.

Any dog, no matter how small, is one of the finest protections for the woman who lives alone. A Pekinese can be as effective as a Great Dane in scaring off an attacker. Rapists don't want to get hurt. Perhaps if they did, they would think twice about raping a woman. They generally don't expect you to resist, but they won't trust your dog.

The problem is that most apartment houses, if they allow pets at all, let you keep only a cat. Cats are fine animals, but they can't bark. If your apartment house has a no-pet rule, draw up a petition with other single tenants and urge the landlord to change this ruling. It's safer for you and ultimately better for the apartment house if tenants are permitted to own dogs.

6
"Self-Protection is the First Law of Nature"
—S. Butler

From the time a female child is old enough to leave the home and venture into the world, she is taught to fear. "Don't take candy from strangers, don't talk to strangers, don't get into a strange car, be careful." Our first lesson in sex education was to fear strangers; strangers who always seemed to be men. We learned to be afraid of rape even before we knew what rape was.

At some point in a woman's life, the things her mother warned her about come true. Perhaps it's a rape or an attempted rape. For many young women, consciousness comes like a thunderclap when an exhibitionist exposes himself. One brief encounter with a sexual pervert burns an indelible mark on a woman's mind. Fear is personified.

However, we were never taught how to react to fear. Women were supposed to be unresisting, passive beings who, when in danger, summon the nearest male. It was normal for a woman to be afraid but highly unnatural for her to do anything about it. This spoon-fed passivity turned women into mental and physical cripples, living proof of the power of negative thinking. "I can't, I shouldn't and I won't." If you tell somebody something long enough, she'll begin to believe it. That's just what happened.

The yardstick which separated the men from the beasts and the "protectors" from the rapists was the code of chivalry. Chivalry was that bastion of male supremacy which determined the proper ways to treat a lady (providing she was one). But this was only a paper pedestal, easily collapsed by a man's arbitrary behavior toward her virtue.

Virtue, in this regard, was a tenuous quality possessed by the chaste woman and revered by any respectable man. This reverence was an admiration for the unknown and the untouched, a healthy respect for the sterling attributes of a woman, assuming that sterling had not tarnished.

History has gone to great lengths to embellish and idealize the "golden age of chivalry," a time when knights were noble and women were pure. The fact is, chivalry wasn't all that chivalrous. A medieval writer, Chrestien de Troyes, explains:

"The usage and rules of that time were that if a knight found a damsel or wench alone, he would, if he wished to preserve his good name, sooner think of cutting his throat than of offering her dishonour; if he forced her against her will he would have been scorned in every court.

"But, on the other hand, if the damsel were accompanied by another knight, and if it pleased him to give combat to that knight and win the lady by arms, then he might do his will with her just as he pleased, and no blame whatsoever would be held to attach him."

And so it went, all the makings of a double

standard. Men force women to be submissive, praise them. The honorable institution of chivalry was responsible for creating the holy trinity of womanhood: oppression, suppression and depression.

But today we are past the time when a damsel in distress need only wave her hand to ferret out the nearest knight on his charger. The modern rapist doesn't follow any code, noble or otherwise.

THE ELEMENT OF SURPRISE

At the outset the rapist has several things in his favor. Since most rapes are planned, the rapist has a script of sorts which he has written, directed and is about to produce. In this script you are his prop, to be manipulated and used in whatever way he sees fit. If the man has raped before (and statistics say he has), he will have had the time to rehearse. Generally a rapist won't deviate from a script that works for him. Some rapists follow the same pattern, approach women in the identical way each time and even say the same words. The Boston Strangler was one of these rapists. His modus operandi, the way he worked, was to scan apartment house mailboxes for female names (first names) and then knock on the door posing as a repairman. He had little trouble gaining entrance into the homes of trusting women.

Not every rapist is as resourceful as the Boston Strangler. Amazingly, some are more so. You *cannot* underestimate the rapist. While it is true that most rapists prefer to follow their premeditated script exactly, some are extremely adaptable. They can handle spontaneous disruptions of their plans, (your scream or the appearance of a witness, for example), and still carry out the act to its intended conclusion, the rape. There are professionals in every field—including rape.

No matter how many times a man has raped before, his role remains the same. He functions as the aggressor, in complete command of the situation. He calls the plays, chooses the victim, location and time, and he doesn't expect you to offer serious resistance. It doesn't enter into his plans. Obviously he doesn't want or expect to be hurt. If he did, he would think about rape in terms of a personal threat with possible consequences instead of an easily executed act.

His sneak attack takes you totally by surprise and the advantage initially belongs to him. However, if you can counter the element of surprise by distracting him or by offering almost any kind of serious resistance (verbal or physical), you may be able to check that advantage and give yourself time to run away. Whenever you throw a wrench into the works which interferes with his plan A, there's a good chance he doesn't have a plan B prepared. Remember, the rapist wants a victim, not an adversary.

YOUR OPTIONS

In some instances, when you're walking down the street and notice that you're being followed, you can change directions and run away. But if he grabs you from behind or enters your home, running isn't enough. You are caught in a situation where you can't run; you're left facing a frighteningly direct confrontation. This gives you two options and one rule. If the man has a weapon, *don't* offer any physical resistance. To do so may result in serious injury or death. No matter how brutal and degrading the rape, it's ultimately better than losing your life.

Your options apply only when the rapist is unarmed. You can freeze and be raped or you can fight back. By fighting back, I don't mean hand-to-hand combat to the death. I mean distracting him only long enough for you to run away.

The major reason for resisting is to give you the needed seconds to get the hell out of there. You may be the type of person who *could* actually stand and beat him to a bloody pulp, but don't. This isn't a duel or boxing match and he certainly isn't observing any formal rules. In fact, he isn't observing any rules but his own. You are facing a sudden, unexpected display of brute force. He catches you off guard and you must do the same to him.

Fright is an "all-systems-breakdown"; it freezes your mind and body. Panic reactions occur when you have no knowledge of what to do and no means with which to do it. Fright leaves you completely immobilized, like a rabbit who, when faced with danger, stops dead in its tracks, leaving itself wide open to be pounced upon. You are unable to move, you can't think rationally and any sounds reaching your ears are muffled as though wrapped in wads of cotton. Panic is caused by a total lack of preparation. You can avoid this mental and physical shutdown by learning to have confidence in yourself. The first hurdle is overcome by realizing that rape *can* happen to you. Be alert to the possibility of being raped *before* the rape occurs. Start by seeing yourself in the unpleasant position of being a victim. Say to yourself, "What would I do, if this happened to me?" Then be aware of those things you *can* do. There *are* options, but to counteract panic effectively, you must take the time to know and practice them.

Courses in karate and self-defense teach the most important lesson of all: self-confidence. It's there all the time, you just have to bring it to the surface. Not every woman is able to enroll in a self-defense class, but it's important to give this option some serious consideration, particularly if your job forces you to walk the streets or take public transportation at night.

Courses in self-defense or karate are given by many universities, Y.W.C.A.'s and some rape crisis centers. Call the ones in your area. If you should decide to enroll in a private karate school, be sure that your instructor is a woman. Women have different problems than men. We are sometimes physically smaller and often psychologically unprepared to protect ourselves. You were born with physical equipment that is more than adequate for defending yourself. You simply have to learn to use it effectively.

The Armed Rapist

If your attacker has a gun or knife, or any weapon, *don't* physically resist him. He may use the weapon against you. The situation now changes from the probability of being raped to the possibility of being killed. It is a life or death decision where the cards have already been laid on the table. To physically resist a man with a gun or knife is senseless and futile. Your best defense in this situation is to try to keep calm. I realize that the likelihood of your remaining calm sounds remote, but you have to keep your head together in order to keep it working.

It's impossible to predict rapists' reactions. They don't fit into any mold and there isn't one pat characterization which applies. However, a rapist with a gun or knife is especially unpredictable and extremely dangerous. My personal advice would be to submit, but memorize his face, the clothes he is wearing and the words he says to you. Afterwards, report every detail to the police. Take your revenge by doing all you possibly can to put the rapist in jail. Don't take the chance of sacrificing your own life.

However, there are some women who have successfully stopped an armed rapist. If you are considering the possibility of doing this yourself, the safest and only thing to do is to try to talk him out of it. Whenever a rapist brandishes a weapon before your face, he doesn't expect you to be calm. He expects and wants you to be afraid of him. In some warped way the rapist finds it exciting and exhilarating. Your fear adds to his feeling of power, of being the dominant male conquering the submissive female.

One word of caution: if the rapist expects and needs a fearful reaction from you, you might be wise to fake fear even if you find yourself feeling surprisingly calm and tempted to resist him. Play along with him; *don't* provoke him under any circumstances. Women who have been raped later admit to feeling shame and humiliation; but the thought uppermost in their minds was a desire to get it over with, to be free of the threat of injury. The victims submitted, they did what the rapist demanded. But, more important, they're alive today to tell about it.

Some women have successfully put their presence-of-mind to clever use. They have, for example, discouraged their attackers by telling them they were infected with gonorrhea, syphilis or a multitude of other contagious diseases. One woman looked her rapist straight in the eyes and said, "I buried my child last week. Somebody hit him with a car and just drove away. He was 10 years old. There's nothing left for me anymore." The man let her go. He didn't know she was unmarried and had never had a child.

Sometimes if you can win the rapist's sympathy and get him to see you as a person with feelings and problems of your own, instead of as an object, you may succeed in stopping the attack. Think about it beforehand. What would you do if confronted by a man with a gun or knife. What could you say which might get his sympathy or stun him. There are infinite possibilities if you use your imagination.

Another woman submitted to an armed rapist but afterwards told the man that she would like to see him again. This Detroit woman gave the rapist her phone number and asked him to call her back. She immediately told the police what she had done and they put a tap on her phone. The hapless rapist, believing he was truly desired, called her back. He was apprehended by the police.

Use this particular ploy only if you are raped in a place *other than your home*. You don't want the rapist returning to your home at any cost. And don't give the man your last name. If he wants to know your name, make one up.

Tactics to win the rapist's sympathy just won't work with some rapists. Schemes such as the ones used by these quick-thinking women may not be successful, in fact may even be dangerous, with your attacker. You can't really plan your reaction ahead of time. For example, one rapist needed to feel that his victims were attracted and sympathetic to him. When the woman tried to talk him out of the attack, he *did* talk, for more than an hour. But afterwards he raped her anyway.

On the other hand, some women have successfully driven off an armed attacker by acting strong and aggressive. One man, who made the mistake of attempting to rape a feisty 73-year-old woman, was shocked when she indignantly screamed "What in heaven's name do you think you're doing, young man" and then proceeded to swat him over the head with her cane. He was so surprised, he ran away.

Although this tactic has worked for some women, it has inflicted others with serious and sometimes fatal injuries. Obviously a man threatening you with a gun or knife is not feeling peaceful and kind at that moment. Showing anger to an armed man may only make him angrier. Don't taunt him.

A very effective scheme is to act crazy. Smile, laugh, say incoherent, ridiculous phrases—anything to catch him off guard. One woman actually grinned at the would-be rapist and declared that she was the Cheshire cat and would he "stay for tea?" This inventive woman so baffled her attacker that he left in a hurry. Think about using this device, since it has a good track record. It's also a fine way to channel and use the hysteria you may be feeling at the time. Try reciting nursery rhymes or even telling jokes, anything to confuse him. Most important, practice it beforehand.

Another means to disconcert attackers is by fainting. A squirming 120 pound woman is far different from 120 pounds of dead weight. By faking a faint you can knock him off balance and give yourself the precious seconds needed to run away. However, use this plan with a healthy amount of caution. If he neglects to catch you and lets you fall to the ground, you'll end up right where he wants you and in trouble.

PLAN AHEAD

Don't wait until the crucial moment when you're face to face with an armed attacker to stop and think of something brilliant to say. Words don't come easily when you're afraid. Keep in mind that one pat set of phrases won't work with every rapist. Have several ideas to draw on. And practice them. They may save you from being raped or killed later.

The Unarmed Rapist

RUN, DON'T WALK

The point of any diversion or self-defense technique is to give you ample time to run away. This *only* applies to an unarmed rapist. Don't run from a man who is carrying a weapon. To do so may startle him and he is apt to use the weapon against you.

Running is your first and best option. But in order to run you have to be wearing clothes which afford you freedom to move quickly. Tight-fitting dresses or ankle-length skirts impede movement. When you're walking on the streets, be sure your clothing won't hinder a getaway. The same applies to your shoes. If you have trouble getting up and down curbs, how do you expect to take off suddenly in a sprint? You can't. If you're wearing platform or other cumbersome shoes, kick them off and run in your bare feet.

Obviously you can run only when your attacker either loosens his grip on you or when you're able to distract him in some way. You have an incredible amount of leverage and a number of options when dealing with an unarmed attacker. But how you ultimately handle yourself depends on the kind of person you are. In order to use some of the weapons and self-defense tactics that will be mentioned, you must see yourself in a position where you are angry enough to hurt the man. You'll have to inflict pain in order to avoid it. This is difficult for some women to envision, but consider the consequences. Rape is a brutal, degrading, humiliating experience. It is a terrifying ordeal which only begins with the act itself and continues through law-enforcement agencies, hospitals and, ultimately, the courts. Aside from the callous, inhumane treatment you may receive from the professionals, rape will change your life. Suddenly you'll be living with constant fear. Fear when you are awake, nightmares when you sleep. It may take years for the terror and dread to subside. For some women, it never ceases. The horror of being raped doesn't go away. It is something you'll live with.

DISTRACTIONS

Anytime you can divert or surprise an unarmed attacker you increase the possibility of snatching the needed seconds to run away. You want to distract him, if only for a minute. You can do this by throwing whatever you happen to be carrying, a magazine, newspaper or package, into the air or in his direction. But *never* throw anything at a man with a weapon.

Note: It is possible, though somewhat unlikely, that a rapist can be carrying a concealed weapon that he will use only if he figures he has to. If a weapon should appear while you're reacting to your attacker as if he were an unarmed rapist, immediately stop your attempts at distraction or running away. Treat him as the unpredictable and dangerous man described under the previous section, The Armed Rapist.

If you don't have something in your hand, you can even pretend to throw something at him. If nothing else, it will startle him so that you can run away. One caution: don't throw out your hands at him for anything more than a split-second. An attacker will try to grab your hands, making escape impossible.

YELLING

Screaming is a fine distraction. Letting loose a blood-curdling yell helps you feel more confident and will probably terrify your attacker. Remem-

ber, the louder you yell, the better. He doesn't expect you to be aggressive. Scream with all the
energy you can muster. Not a frightened, whimper-
ing cry, but a powerful, angry yell. Don't hesitate
to shout obscenities. You're not auditioning for
the church choir, you're preventing a rape.

When you take a deep breath, the abdominal
muscles tighten. This contraction increases the
power of your physical self-defense tactics (an elbow to the abdomen, a kick to the shins etc.). An
angry, strong yell forces the air out like a shotgun
blast. Practice it. You'll be surprised how terrifying it sounds.

THE FREON HORN

The freon or air horn can take over if and when
your voice fails you. It's a cylinder about three
inches tall attached to a plastic horn on top. This
mini-wonder lets out an incredibly shrill, ear-split-
ting blast which actually can shatter the rapist's
eardrum if you hold it close to his face. You also
can remove the plastic horn attachment in a matter of seconds and squirt the chemical into his
eyes. Freon is a freezing agent which causes temporary blindness, giving you time to run and get
help.

The freon or air horn is light, weighing about
two ounces, and fits comfortably into your hand.
It's a great companion when you walk the streets
at night or use the subway. The horn is also effective in discouraging obscene phone callers. You

can buy freon horns at most sporting-goods and hardware stores for about $2.50. Refills cost about $1.00. If you are a member of a woman's club or other organization, you probably will be able to purchase them by bulk at a discount.

The Freon Horn

POLICE WHISTLES

Police whistles are another good investment for deterring rapists. The whistle has a twofold advantage: it can be heard at great distances and it sounds like a call from a police officer in trouble. The best place to carry a police whistle is on a chain around your neck. They can be bought at most sporting-goods stores for about $1.50.

MACE

The most commonly sold mace is a small cylinder which can be carried in your pocketbook. But it's often more dangerous for you than to your attacker. Since it's the same size as a breath freshener or a purse-sized can of hairspray, many women have inadvertently maced themselves. Furthermore, this type of mace doesn't squirt very far and must be used only when the wind is at your back. Otherwise both you and the would-be rapist suffer the same effects. It's ridiculous to think that while you're being threatened with attack you have time to wet your index finger and poke it in the air to see which way the wind is blowing and, if it happens to be blowing the wrong way, ask the rapist to please turn around so you can mace him. This kind of mace may be purchased at any store and I suggest you stay away from it.

Another type of mace is offered by some police departments. The container is larger and heavier, about the size of a deodorant can. The force of the aerosol is infinitely more powerful than the purse-sized can but the same precautions must be observed when using it. Mace is composed of a liquid tear gas and a kerosene-based chemical which adheres to the skin when sprayed. In a heavy wind the spray will change directions and waft across your face. Unless you happen to be wearing a gas mask, mace is dangerous and should not be used for protection.

TEAR-GAS GUNS

Several states prohibit tear-gas guns with good reason. First of all, tear gas can be lethal to people who have heart problems and serious respiratory conditions. The gas doesn't discriminate between attacker and victim. Also, tear-gas guns are prone to what is called a "blow-back" effect. The term "blow-back effect" is suitably self-descriptive. One good breeze in your direction and you receive more tear gas than your attacker. In addition, innocent bystanders have been partially blinded because fragments of the shell which encases the gas shattered and spread like minute pieces of glass. Don't use these guns; they are extremely hazardous.

Weapons

It's illegal to carry a gun on the street without a permit. In the hands of an untrained person, a handgun is your worst enemy. Many women buy guns and keep them in their bedrooms. If you have a gun either go to your local police station or enroll in a gun club and learn how to use it safely and properly. There is another unforseeable problem with having a gun in your home. A 16-year-old boy, depressed because of low grades on his report card, took the handgun from the night table of his parents' bedroom, put it to his head and pulled the trigger. In other instances, what began as a marital argument ended in murder. Guns are dangerous.

The purpose of using weapons and fighting back is to give you ample time to run away. You are not acting in the final scene from *High Noon*, you are buying time.

A word of caution. According to the law, in defending yourself you can use force only of sufficient intensity to repel your attacker. Excessive force could result in your being prosecuted on criminal charges. The point is, your self-defense cannot exceed the amount of force or the threat of injury exhibited by the would-be rapist. This legal concept exists to protect innocent people from indiscriminate harm.

One woman walking down a city street at night noticed she was being followed by a man. He caught up with her and put his hand on her shoulder to stop her. In her mind he was a rapist. Pulling a pocket knife from her purse, she stabbed him in the chest. The man was taken to the hospital, the woman to jail. The man had intended merely to ask directions, not to rape her. The woman was charged with several crimes, among them assault with a deadly weapon. The man had not harmed her or threatened her with bodily harm. Under the law her overreaction to the situation resulted in her criminal prosecution.

PRACTICAL WEAPONS

Hat pins Though out of style for the fashion-conscious woman, a sturdy two-inch hat pin is still the most effective legal weapon. But in order to be helpful, the pin belongs in your hand, not in your pocketbook. You can also keep it within reach, pinned to the outside of your clothes.

There are two ways to hold a hat pin. Choose the one with which you feel most comfortable. You can hold it between your thumb and forefinger, keeping a good, strong grip on it. The pin has a small knob on the end which looks like a pearl. If you have trouble getting a secure grip, try wrapping some plastic tape around the knob. The tape gives you more to hold on to.

An alternative is to place the pin in the palm of your hand near the base of the fingers. Position the knob between the index and middle fingers, then make a fist. The point should stick out about one-quarter to one-half of an inch from your fist.

If the time comes when you are forced to use the hat pin on an attacker, remember, you want to hurt him. Jab at any exposed area, face, hands, neck, arm, etc., and as soon as he eases his grip on you, run away.

Hat pins can be bought at any department or millinery store and cost about 20¢.

Plastic lemon Plastic lemons are a bit bulkier to carry around than hat pins, but they do a fine job. You can buy the lemons at any food store. You might prefer to screw off the top of the lemon and replace the juice with ammonia, detergent or liquid insecticide. Aim for the eyes. The lemon can squirt up to 15 feet.

Lighted cigarette Smash the cigarette into the attacker's eyes, face, hands or arm in the same way you would put out your cigarette in an ashtray.

Umbrella Place one hand near the center, underneath the umbrella and your other hand toward the back, on top. Jab quickly and forcefully into the man's abdomen.

Corkscrew The corkscrew easily penetrates the soft, fleshy areas of the body. Pierce, then twist.

Magazine or newspaper Roll it into a tube and strike on the bridge of the nose, neck, arm or any exposed area.

Hard-bound book Hold the book with both hands and smash it directly on his nose. You also can deliver an effective one-handed blow by hitting him on the side of the neck with the edge of the book.

Fork The ordinary kitchen fork can be used like a three-pronged dagger. Stab or rake it across any exposed area.

Hairbrush or comb Get a solid grip and rake or slash it across his face, neck, throat or any exposed area.

Pen, pencil or metal fingernail file Use like a dagger and stab at his face or neck.

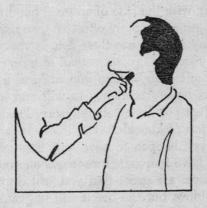

Pocketbook The purse, used by itself, can be a weapon. Hold it tightly in both hands and smash it into his face, nose or throat. Don't swing your purse unless you intend to let go of it. He may try to grab it and you'll lose your balance.

Besides being a weapon in its own right, your pocketbook contains many articles you can use to defend yourself.

Keys Grasp the key chain in the palm of your hand and let one key stick out between every finger. Use it to scrape across the neck, face or back of his hand. Don't punch, this isn't a pair of brass knuckles and the impact will drive the keys into the palm of your hand.

Self-Defense Techniques

The Open-hand Blow

Striking with the side of an open hand requires less strength and is more effective than using your fists. Many women use their fists as though they were knocking on a door instead of trying to land a good hard blow. When you make a fist, your wrist may have a tendency to wilt and lean forward. What you have left is a sorry-looking conglomeration of knuckles attached to a very weak base. If you happen to have long fingernails you also will have four puncture marks on your palm. The chances are great that you will draw blood by your blow, but the blood will be yours. Don't use your fists; use the side of your open hand instead.

In order to be effective you have to keep your fingers together, bending them very slightly, and cup the palm of your hand just a bit. Always keep your thumb glued to the side of your index finger, not folded into your palm. The thumb acts like a vise and cements the rest of your fingers together, giving you a powerful, streamlined weapon.

Whenever you use the open-hand blow, be sure to hit with the wad of muscle just below the little finger. Striking in this way cushions your hand while increasing the force of the blow. Never hit with your fingers; you'll find that the little finger is suddenly next to your thumb. It will be very painful and very broken. The same warning applies to your wrist. The wrist is composed of bone covered by a thin layer of skin. One quick, hard jab will be enough to shatter the bone, leaving you in excruciating pain.

To get the feel of the open-hand blow, practice by gently hitting the fleshy part of the side of your hand on a table top. You can gradually increase the force of the blows without feeling any pain.

The best way to practice the open-hand blow is

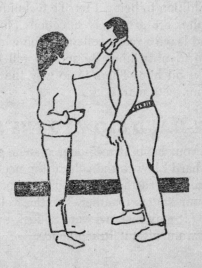

with a partner, particularly a man. Using him will help you gauge the height difference while getting you accustomed to a moving target. There's no need to be overly dramatic while practicing—just lightly touch the pressure point areas.

THE TEETH

One of the finest self-defense weapons is located in your mouth and doesn't require any training to use. If he grabs you with his arm or attacks you from behind with a bear hug, chomp down on any part of his arm. The best place to set your teeth is in the pad of soft flesh between his thumb and index finger (assuming you're in a position to reach it). One good bite into this area can paralyze his hand and he'll be forced to let you go.

In addition to being a terrific technique, human teeth bites are extremely infectious (for the rapist) and leave a red, swollen outline which can be used to identify him. Be sure to tell the police that you bit him. There is no way the rapist can hide your teeth marks.

OPEN-HAND BLOW TO THE NECK

Aim your hand at a 45-degree angle and give a sharp, hard blow to the side of the neck. Be sure to strike with the fleshy part of your hand and to keep your fingers together. Practice yelling when you hit. It may feel awkward at first, but will become natural after a little practice.

OPEN-HAND BLOW TO THE NOSE

When practicing this defense, gently touch your partner's nose, but in reality use a strong,

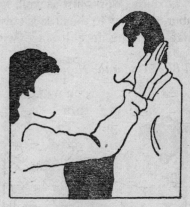

The Open-Hand Blow to the Neck

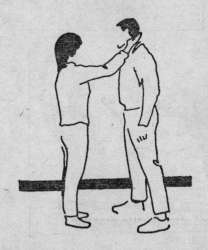

smashing blow. You should strike on a downward
angle directly across the bridge of the nose. Also
practice open-hand blows under the nose and
remember, a hard-bound book, a hefty paperback
or a bag of groceries works just as well.

Remember, the blow to the nose is only effective
when you're standing face to face with an at-

Open-hand Blow Under the Nose

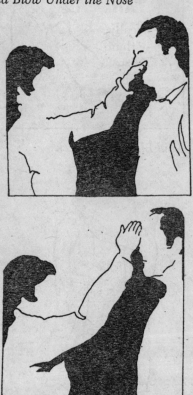

tacker in close quarters. It's useless and dangerous when he is more than six inches away from you.

Also practice open-hand blows upward, under the chin; a diagonal slash to the solar plexus; to the windpipe (be careful in rehearsals, the windpipe is delicate); across the shoulder muscle and to the forearm, inner elbow and wrist.

THE OPEN-HAND STAB

This stab is basically the same as the open-hand blow except the thumb is spread so that your hand forms a V. Curve your fingers slightly and use a snapping motion. A jabbing blow causes extreme pain and is also effective on the throat.

The Open-hand Stab

THE HEEL OF THE PALM BLOW

Cup your hand, fingers together and thumb in. Strike upward under the chin with the heel of

Heel of the Palm Blow

your palm (not your fingers). This is a powerful blow when done sharply and also can be used under the nose. Striking with the heel of the palm will send your attacker reeling and is excellent for close-quarters combat.

THE ELBOW BLOW

The elbow blow is a good way to defend yourself against an attack from the rear. However, if he pins your arms tightly against the side of your body, you will have little room to maneuver. In this case, try a kick to his shin with the heel of your foot.

If your arm is somewhat free, spread your feet apart for better balance and drive your elbow into his solar plexus, abdomen or chin. Taking a deep breath and yelling at the same time increases the force of the blow.

The Elbow Blow

THE KICK

Kicking effectively isn't difficult but it does require some practice. The best way to achieve accuracy is to suspend a hard rubber ball (drill a hole in the center and insert a rope through it, tie at one end) about knee-high and try to hit the target with your foot. You also can set up a stationary target (seat cushion or mattress) and visualize one point that you want to hit.

Move your feet so that the side of your body is facing the target and bend your left leg for balance. Lift up your right leg (knee bent) and kick the target with the outside of your foot right below your toes. Snap it back quickly to regain your balance. You may be unsuccessful at your first few attempts to hit the mark but your improvement will be amazing. Practice kicking with either foot.

The Kick

To practice kicking a man who attacks you from the rear, prop a seat cushion or mattress against the wall and stand about two to three feet away. Bend your left leg for balance and snap your right leg quickly and hit the cushion with the heel of your foot. In the case of back kicks, mark off two points; one for the shin and the other for the kneecap. The back kick should be one continuous motion. A short snappy kick, then lean forward so that your movement points you in the proper direction for running away.

The quality of your kick depends entirely on the kind of shoes you wear. Kicking with platform shoes or soft sandals is ineffective.

Remember, the best kicks are low kicks to the

kneecap and shin. Always kick with your knee
bent and strike hard with the heel of your foot.
You want to develop a quick, stamping kick. This
will immobilize your attacker long enough for you
to run away.

As with every self-defense technique, scream
while you are kicking. It will increase the force of
the kick.

THE FRONT-CHOKE DEFENSE

The attacker faces you and wraps his fingers
around your neck. Raise your arms, dig your fingers into the soft flesh of his inner elbow. This is
the weakest part of his grip and his pain will force
him to release you.

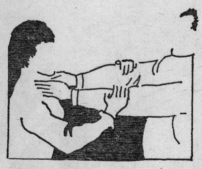

The Front-choke Defense

ATTACKS FROM THE REAR

The attacker grabs you from behind and pins
your arms against the side of your body. This is a

common attack. If you intend to kick with your right foot, bend your left knee for balance and smash the heel of your right foot into his shin. Just as soon as you feel his grip loosen, run away.

The attacker wraps his forearm around your neck, choking you. To relieve the pressure on your windpipe, *turn your head toward his elbow,* grab his choking arm with both hands and jerk it downward. Do it with one quick, hard snap.

Your throat is gripped from behind, his fingers pressing into your windpipe. Grab his little fingers and pull them back as hard as you can. The little fingers are vulnerable since they aren't used for gripping and aren't strong. Pulling on them is very painful and will make him let go. Run away.

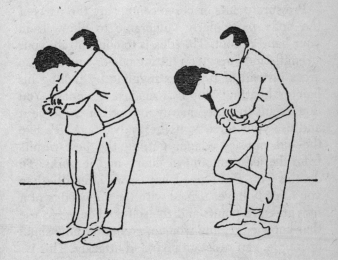

Pressure Points

Pressure points or nerve centers are the parts of the body particularly vulnerable to blows from your hand or foot. The idea is to concentrate your strength and energy on hitting one or two of these areas instead of futilely struggling by pulling his hair or beating your fists against his chest. You don't want to waste energy, but rather conserve it and use your force to its best advantage. It's like the old physics adage: getting the best results from the least amount of effort—and it works. To do this you don't need any more strength than you already have. Armed with the knowledge of a few pressure points and the self-confidence to use that knowledge, any woman, no matter how small or fragile, can resist an unarmed attacker.

The nose—The nose is a tremendous place to land a blow. Any strike to the nose is extremely painful and will cause his eyes to tear like a waterfall. Smashing the nose with the side of your open hand or book will stun him and a hard blow may render him unconscious for several minutes.

Hitting up under the nose has the same effect. He also will be left with two black eyes easily identifiable in a police line-up. The nose is a prime target providing you are close enough to reach it. Don't flail your arm wildly into the air trying to get a shot at the rapist's nose. He could grab your arm and you'd be in a worse position. Smash the nose only when you are in close quarters and don't attempt it unless one of your arms is free.

The ear—A moderate blow to the ear is painful but

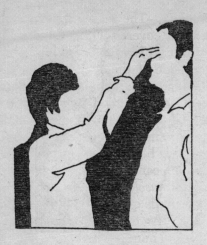

this area isn't as good as the nose or the side of the neck.

Under the jaw—This is the fleshy area underneath the jaw bone, not the jaw itself. Cupping your hand and striking this area with the fingertips is painful. Again, this is effective only when you're close to the man.

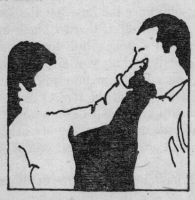

Side of the neck—The neck is a tremendous target area. It's rarely covered by clothing, and it doesn't take a forceful blow to cause sharp pain. You can hit the side of the neck with an open-hand blow from any angle: when he's in front of you, at your side, or in back of you.

The windpipe—Even the softest blow to the windpipe causes tremendous pain, often choking the attacker. A hard blow to this area with the side of your open hand can be fatal.

The shoulder muscle—This is a good target area located at the base of the neck between the collarbone and neck. An open-hand blow is painful and a hard blow will numb his arm for a short while.

The hollow of the throat—The throat is an extremely vulnerable area located underneath the windpipe. Stabbing with clenched fingertips or

jabbing the hollow of the throat with your thumb can result in serious injury and may be fatal.

The solar plexus—The solar plexus is the fleshy area just below where the ribs part and is a good place to use your elbow, open hand or umbrella. When you hit straight into the solar plexus, it knocks the wind out of him, doubling him up like a pretzel. One good shot into this area produces intense pain and will immobilize the rapist long enough for you to run away.

The lower abdomen—A swift elbow to this area can double up your attacker.

Inside the elbow joint—A sharp, snappy blow with your open hand to the inside of his elbow is painful and will force your attacker to loosen his grip.

The forearm—The forearm is the mass of muscle located just beneath the elbow. A moderate blow

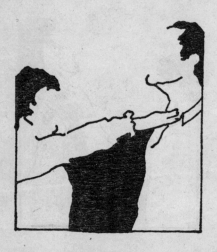

to the forearm is painful and a sharp, forceful blow will numb the arm.

The wrist—A sharp, open-hand blow to the wrist causes pain and will loosen his grip on your arm or neck.

The back of the hand—Rake a comb, key, corkscrew, pen, pencil or fork across the back of his hand. You also can dig your fingernails or teeth into the thin veil of skin. This part of his hand is virtually unprotected and frequently exposed during the attack.

Fingers—If a man grabs you, take hold of his little finger and pull it back. It's the most vulnerable and accessible finger since it isn't used for gripping.

The groin—Never aim first for the groin. The rapist knows what a kick or knee to the groin can do to

him far better than you. It's the first place he protects. Forget what you've been told about the groin being the bulls-eye and choose another less protected area for your initial attack.

Inner thigh—The inner thigh is not a good target area since it's only reached by a high kick which will throw you off balance. Unless you have been schooled in the fine techniques of karate, forget it.

The knee—This is one of the best target areas for self-defense. Any kick to the knee causes pain and a forceful one throws the man off balance and can dislocate the knee. It doesn't take any special skill or training for an effective knee kick.

The shin—Aim for the shin whenever you can. Right below the surface of the shin is an extensive concentration of nerves totally unprotected by any muscle. A quick snap kick to the shin is extremely painful.

The ankle—A hard kick to the ankle with the side of your shoe is effective when the man is close to

you. A sharp kick to the angle bone is painful and will cause him to lose his balance.

The instep—Stamping on his instep with the heel of your shoe causes tremendous pain and a hard kick can shatter the small bones in the arch of his foot.

PRESSURE POINTS ON THE BACK OF THE BODY

These points are the most accessible areas during an attack:

The kidney—Put your hands on your hips. The area near your thumbs is where the kidneys are located. The kidneys are extremely vulnerable and a moderate open-hand blow or punch produces sharp, severe pain.

Back of the knee—This is an excellent area for self-defense tactics. A sharp kick to the back of the knee will throw the man off balance.

The calf—A quick, hard kick to the calf numbs the leg and is painful.

The Achilles' heel or tendon—This is a grossly overrated area unless you're wearing shoes with cleats. The tendon is amply protected by the man's shoes. Land a hard kick to the calf instead.

7
The Rape

"I felt so dirty—filthy. I took a shower and let the hot water hit me, but I couldn't touch myself. My own body was revolting, disgusting. I just stood there crying, holding a washcloth in my hand, but I couldn't touch myself. God, how I wanted to go down the drain with the rest of the water."

A Boston rape victim

"For months afterwards, every face was his face. When the telephone rang, I sat there watching it, but couldn't pick it up. He seemed to be everywhere, even when I closed my eyes."

A New Jersey rape victim

"He was only a boy, younger than my own son. What would he want with a 43-year-old woman? I'm 43 years old. . . . My God, why me?"

A Philadelphia rape victim

". . . I'll tell you one thing, if that ever happens again I'll kill the bastard . . . I never dreamed I could say it, but it's true. I'd rather die than have to go through that again."

A New Jersey rape victim

Rape.

The American Heritage Dictionary definition: "The crime of forcing a female to submit to sexual intercourse."

The legal definition: "Carnal knowledge through the use of force or the threat of force."—*FBI Uniform Crime Reports*.

Rape.

One word doesn't begin to explain or describe the emotions of a woman who has been forcibly raped. Dictionary and legal definitions don't come close.

It's a time when everything you believed in, everything you thought was true about yourself, about the world, is now suddenly a lie. The person staring back at you in the mirror is a stranger. The person you always thought you were no longer exists.

Then there is the fear. Fear of dying, of realizing in an instant that you aren't immortal, that you never were. Fear of being alone, of being in crowds, of men . . . all men. Fear of your husband, family or friends finding out. The fear of being raped again. The nightmares, the obsession with rape.

How can you possibly tell anyone what happened and will they believe you? You're not sure of yourself anymore. You're self-conscious, embarrassed and confused. Other women are raped, not me; it wasn't me. But it was and you're empty and alone.

Sometimes the embarrassment turns to guilt.

Guilt is anger with no place to go, so you turn it against yourself. Why did this happen to me, what did I do? Could I have stopped it? Will I ever be able to have a normal sex life? Will my husband or lover think it was my fault?

Later there's anger, perhaps the most blessed relief for you. Be angry, angry with the rapist. Angry enough to do something about it, to see that the man pays, to fight back.

The decision to report your rape to the police is a personal one. You must decide for yourself. No one is going to force or coerce you into reporting if you don't want to. It won't be the easiest thing for you to do. In fact, it'll be difficult. You will be asked intimate and endless questions about the rape and at times you'll feel as though you're the one on trial, not the rapist. It's a difficult and often prolonged procedure. In a sense you'll be subjected to another kind of attack; this one from the public officials whose purpose *should* be to help, not hurt. Their prodding and digging exaggerate the details of a private horror you'd rather forget. In a sense, it's like being raped all over again.

Never forget that you have the right to know what's going on and why. Why certain questions and procedures are necessary and why they are being carried out. You also should be aware of those frequent questions asked of you which are irrelevent and should not be answered. It's your right and obligation to know and understand just what happens when you report a rape: the whole painful procedure from police and hospitals to the courts.

If rape is to be seen as something more than a locker-room joke, *it must be reported.* It's the only way. Legislation can't be changed until the appalling frequency of the crime is made known. Laws won't be rewritten for a crime whose statistics are only estimates. At present only one out of ten women who are raped report the act. We have to take rape out of the closet. For centuries rapists have had their own way and we've given them our silent blessing to continue to rape with impunity. One reported rape, your rape, will matter.

Through all the procedural difficulties, the feelings of harassment and the courtroom embarrassments, try as hard as you can to remember that the point of all this is to satisfy your personal anger and discourage future rapes. You'll be going through an ordeal beyond the ordeal of the rape itself with one goal in mind: to find, convict and punish the dangerous individual who raped you. Pursue that goal relentlessly with all the strength you possess.

Stop feeling guilty and start feeling angry. You have been used, defiled, degraded and humiliated. Don't cry rape, scream it.

IF YOU ARE RAPED

Call the police immediately and tell them you were raped, then call a friend or neighbor and tell her or him what happened. Tell your friend everything you can remember about the rapist and the details of the rape. This is important; you have just gone through a tremendously horrifying experience and you may forget to tell some things to the police. It may take five minutes or an hour for a squad car to arrive, so it's imperative to relate the details to another person while they are still fresh in your mind. It's normal at this point to be in a state of shock. It doesn't seem real to you yet and you may find it easier to talk about what happened, even if it seems as if your account is in the third person. The fact that it was *you* who's been raped may not have sunk in yet. The call to your friend also can be admitted as evidence in your court case.

If your town's police department has a Rape Squad or a Sex Crime Squad, officers from the Squad will arrive in answer to your call. Hopefully they will be women. But if you know that your area has a Rape Crisis Center and/or a rape hot line, call that number after phoning the police. The women at Rape Crisis Centers will give you, at this crucial moment, invaluable help—both practical advice and emotional support. Often one of these women will come pick you up and go with you to the hospital and police precinct. She'll help you face your immediate problems, whether they're as simple as canceling your commitments for the next day or as complex as coping with your family's reaction. Many times the Crisis Center woman who helps you is a woman who also has been raped. She's always a woman who's concerned about your feelings and understands your fears. She's helped others like you and she can take some of the immediate weight of "what do I do next" off your shoulders onto hers.

Your first and most natural impulse will be to wash or douche. *Don't.* The sorry truth is that you are a walking, breathing piece of evidence and nothing on your body should be touched. Washing may destroy semen if any is present. A special test for sperm is done during the medical examination and the result of the test is used in your court case.

Leave on the clothes you were wearing at the time, don't change them. They may contain traces of the man's blood or semen. If the rape occurred in a home or apartment, leave everything just the way it was at the time of the rape. If a table or chair was knocked over, don't pick it up or touch it. It may have the rapist's fingerprints on it and it is a sign of a struggle, which the policemen will note.

If you are physically able, make mental and written notes of exactly what happened. How did the rapist approach you; did he come through the door, window, did he meet you on the street, get out of a car, etc.? Try to remember all you can about the rapist. What he looked like, his height, his clothes. Most important, try to recall what the rapist said to you, if anything. It's possible and probable that the man who raped you has raped before and he very likely will use the same words or phrases each time. This information is extremely essential in helping the police identify the man. The police department has files on sex offenders and the files contain a record of the words used by the rapists.

Normally two police officers answer your call for help. They may seem cold and callous toward you; rape calls are routine for them. You may never have been raped before but they have answered numerous rape calls and have learned to treat each one in a cold, objective manner. They are not there to judge whether or not a rape was committed; they are there to ask you explicit questions about the rapist and the rape. Some questions are intimate and may seem unnecessary or unimportant to you. However they must be asked.

Besides getting a physical description of the man, the policemen have to know everything about his Modus Operandi (MO). The MO is the rapist's script; it's how he operates. Remember, chances are this man has raped other women and the rapist generally doesn't deviate from his basic script. He usually says the exact same words, threatens or approaches women in the same way. The more information and help you give to the police, the better the chances of getting this man off the streets.

Police Questioning

If you were raped in your home, two police officers come to your house to ask you questions. If you were raped on the street or in a car, the police pick you up and drive to the precinct in the district where the rape occurred.

The initial police questioning is fairly standard in every city. The policemen ask you questions and write down your answers. They then file a report of the incident at the precinct. Just tell them the truth to the best of your recollection. If you don't understand a question, ask for an explanation and if you want to add something to any of your answers, be sure to speak up.

The police officer is generally very thorough in his interrogation. He must write a report and, if you should decide to prosecute, he will appear in court to testify to exactly what happened when you spoke with him.

You probably will be asked: What time did the attack occur and why didn't you call the police immediately? Had you ever seen the assailant (rapist) before? If so, how did you know him? What did he look like? (height, weight, color of hair, skin, approximate age) Did he have any unusual facial features? (scars, tattoos, moles) Did he have a weapon and what was it? Did he threaten you and how? Did he speak with an accent? What did he say before, during and after the attack? Did he use obscenities and what were they? Did you resist and how did you resist? Did he undress and what did he take off? Did you notice anything unusual about his genital or other not-visible area? Did you undress, what did you take off? Did he hit or beat you? Did he penetrate? Did he have a climax? Did he steal anything and is anything missing? How did he leave and in what direction did he go? If you were raped in the street near a car or in a car, you're asked to describe the model, color and approximate year of the car.

It is also routine procedure to ask about any abnormal acts which might have occurred during the rape. The police have a checklist of abnormal acts which they read to you. These questions may sound voyeuristic but the police must ask them. They are trying to put together the rapist from your description and it's necessary that they cover every aspect of the rape. Tell the police everything you can remember, no matter how intimate or embarrassing the details.

The categories on the checklist of abnormal acts are: Sodomy (penis into anus); Defecation; Urination; Sadism; Masochism; Put Object into Vagina; Set Fire to Victim; Photographed Victim; Tongue or Mouth to Anus; Put Hand into Vagina; Talked About Body Functions; Multiple Victims; Multiple Rapes. Just tell the police the truth, don't hold anything back.

There are some policemen who have been known to go above and beyond the call of duty when questioning a rape victim. These are people who get their kicks by asking irrelevant questions about the rape. You do not have to answer these questions. Were you really raped, or are you just trying to get back at the man? Did you lead him on? How did you feel? Did you enjoy it? Did you have a climax? Don't answer.

If you notice any cuts or bruises on your body, show them to the policeman. In addition to the details you have already given, the police make a note of your overall condition on their report. They write down whether you were calm, hysterical, shaken, in a daze, angry, etc. They also note any torn clothing, cuts, bruises, etc.

If you remember scratching the rapist's face or any part of his body, tell the police. It's quite possible that you might have bits of his skin under your fingernails. The policeman will take a scraping from underneath the nails and send it to the police laboratory for examination. If you pulled off a button or tore the man's clothes, tell them. If the rapist had an orgasm, the police will ask for your underpants so that they can be sent to the lab and analyzed for semen or blood stains.

Also be sure to tell the police if you called a friend or neighbor after the rape. They will question your friend to see if she or he knows any details which you might have forgotten.

Should you be badly injured, the police will take you immediately to the hospital. Otherwise, they first may take you to the police station in the precinct where the rape occurred. There you're asked to give another description of the man who attacked you so the police can put out an All-Points Bulletin (APB) over the police radios to catch the man as soon as possible. If you were beaten or bruised, photographs might be taken for use as evidence in a court case.

This interview is very brief. The police then drive you to the hospital for a medical examination.

The Hospital

The standard medical examination given to a rape victim is to ensure and prove several things. First the woman is treated for any injury she may have received during the rape. The second purpose, although not immediately necessary to the woman who has been raped less than several hours prior to the examination, is to gain evidence for building a case against the rapist should she want to prosecute. The third function of the examination is to test and treat her for venereal disease and to take measures against becoming pregnant.

The most important and perhaps the most neglected part of the medical examination is regard for the emotions of a woman who has just been forcibly raped. More than a bandage, or medication or an internal examination, the rape victim needs compassion, not judgment or sterile treatment. She is different from other emergency-ward cases. She has just come from a degrading, humiliating experience. At this point, she may feel as though she has lost every shred of personal privacy. And at the hospital she may feel she is losing some more.

*"First they couldn't take me to the hospital
across the street from the police station because
the cop said they didn't take rape cases. Here I
am, my eye's swollen so I can't see and they're
driving me cross country to a hospital."*

A Massachusetts rape victim

Most private hospitals won't accept rape victims, so the woman is taken to the nearest hospital
that does or to the city general hospital. Some
states require the attending physician to appear
in court and testify as to what was done and
found in the medical examination. Many doctors
are reluctant to take time away from their prac-
tices to testify in court. If the hospital doesn't
treat rape cases, it eliminates the need for the
doctor to appear. It's that simple. And because
there's a great deal of red tape and legal compli-
cations in handling rape cases, many hospitals shy
away from treating women who have been raped.

So you can't choose which hospital to go to because many of them don't want you. You also
have no choice in the kind of treatment you receive once you get there. Some hospital personnel
show no special consideration for rape victims;
they can be amazingly insensitive.

*"So they finally get me to the hospital and I'm
waiting. As a matter of fact, the cop and myself
are sitting next to a guy with a broken arm and
they take him before they take me . . . Two
hours later the doctor comes out and asks where*

the "rape" is. He takes one look at my eye and asks me if I ran into a wall . . . Oh, I can talk about it now, but I'll tell you, I was crying the whole time."

Very often a woman is seen and examined by an intern or resident who has had little training in the gentle art of being humane to rape victims. Sometimes the number of cuts and bruises on a woman's body is the doctor's personal criterion for judging if the woman has been raped.

"The doctor asked if I had been beaten. I said no. He told me to go home. That it wasn't worth it."

A New York rape victim

In some cities and suburbs, a police officer accompanies the woman to the hospital and stays in the examining room with her. New York and Washington D.C., to name two cities, have special Sex Crime Squads which send a police*woman* to escort the rape victim during the medical examination. There is a reason for this invasion of privacy: the police need to witness the procedures performed by the doctor, the tests made, what was done with the lab samples, etc. But unfortunately, the feeling you are left with is that you're a piece of evidence to be probed, talked about and recorded for official purposes.

Often the medical examination itself is a mystery to you. Few doctors take the time to explain what they are doing and why.

THE WAY IT CAN BE

Since its founding in May, 1973, the Philadelphia Women Organized Against Rape (WOAR) has instigated tremendous changes in the treatment of the rape victim in Philadelphia. Their group is a model of the results that can be achieved when rape crisis center and institutions work together. WOAR is situated at 1220 Sansom St., 11th floor, Phila., Pa. 19107.

Before the advent of WOAR, rape victims waited in the emergency room along with other emergency cases and no special consideration was shown to them. Now, Presbyterian Hospital and Jefferson Hospital have set aside special waiting and examining rooms where the women can wait in privacy with their families and friends who have accompanied them to the hospital.

As soon as the rape victim arrives at the hospital, a clerk calls the WOAR office and a volunteer arrives within minutes, wearing a blue blazer signifying that she is a WOAR member. The volunteer greets the woman by saying "Hi, my name is Mary and I'm here to help you." She is there to lend emotional support to the rape victim, not to ask questions. The victim is given a copy of her legal and medical rights and the volunteer explains the medical examination and the medications she will receive. The rape victim is given a card with the telephone number of the organization's 24-hour hotline and the volunteer asks the woman if she would like someone to call her back several days later to make sure that everything is all right.

As with all rape crisis centers, the personal needs of the rape victim are of the utmost concern to WOAR. The organization works closely with Presbyterian and Jefferson Hospitals and the hospitals' personnel has been cooperative and compassionate in humanizing the hospital ordeal for the rape victim. WOAR also conducts training sessions with the gynecological residents and nurses, dealing with the psychological needs of a woman who has been raped. Due to the cooperation of Presbyterian and Jefferson Hospitals and the efforts of WOAR to bring about changes, the waiting time for the internal examination has been reduced drastically. If the woman waits longer than 75 minutes, the hospital director is alerted.

Gradually more and more hospitals are making significant efforts to improve the treatment of the rape victim. The rape crisis centers are responsible for making less callous and indifferent the handling of frightened, embarrassed women. Professionals are now doing their best to treat the rape victim with insight and sympathy. The treatment often extends beyond the medical examination. Rap groups and counseling sessions are available to help the woman and her family understand what has happened.

The Medical Examination

The doctor should begin by taking a brief medical history. Have you ever had any pelvic diseases, infections or operations? What type of birth control do you use, if any? What was the date of your last menstrual period? Is your period regular and how many days does it last? Is your flow heavy and do you have cramps?

He or she then asks you detailed questions about every aspect of the rape. What time were you raped? What did he do? For the second time you have to relive every moment of the rape. Be frank and honest with the doctor, tell him everything that happened. If you were forced to engage in anal or oral sex, be sure to mention it. It's important in treating you for venereal disease.

The germs which cause gonorrhea and syphilis are transmitted by any contact with a mucous membrane of the body. Put a clean finger into your mouth and touch the inside of your cheek right now. That's a mucous membrane. It's soft, wet and warm. These same types of membranes line the vagina, penis, throat and anus. If the rapist has a venereal disease and his penis comes in contact with your mouth or anus, you can be infected there. It's imperative to tell the doctor so that you're given the proper medication.

The doctor also asks when you last had intercourse with your husband or boyfriend. The doctor isn't prying into your personal life. He or she will perform a sperm test for legal purposes. If the rapist ejaculated, sperm will be present in your vagina for up to 24 hours. This is used as evidence in a court case. The defense lawyer (representing the rapist) may attempt to prove that the sperm was the remains of consenting intercourse prior to the rape, not the result of the rape. So it's necessary that the doctor has this information to testify in your behalf at the trial.

The doctor writes on his or her report everything you mentioned about the rape using your own words. He or she also notes your general physical condition, appearance and emotional state at the time of the examination. The physician also notes any cuts, bruises or lacerations and any torn or bloody clothing.

THE EXTERNAL EXAMINATION

You're given a hospital gown and asked to undress. As you lie on your back on the examining table, the doctor checks the surface of your body and external genital organs for any bruises, cuts, scrapes or lacerations. If you recall the man grabbing you around the neck or holding you tightly in any area, tell the doctor. He or she will examine the area for bruises or redness (trauma).

THE INTERNAL OR PELVIC EXAMINATION

As you lie on your back with your legs propped up in stirrups, the doctor inserts a water-moist-

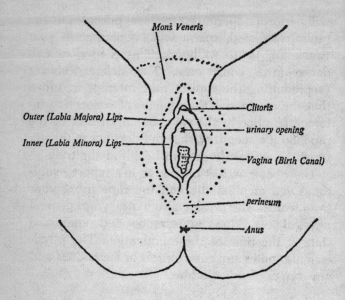

Mons Veneris

Outer (Labia Majora) Lips —

Inner (Labia Minora) Lips —

— Clitoris

— urinary opening

— Vagina (Birth Canal)

— perineum

— Anus

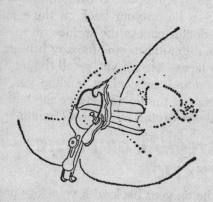

Use of the Speculum

ened speculum into your vagina. A speculum is
an instrument made of plastic or metal which
holds the vaginal walls apart so the doctor can get
a clear view of your cervix. The cervix is a narrow,
muscular tube extending from the uterus (womb)
into the vagina. The opening from the cervix to
the vagina is called the cervical canal. This canal
is made up of a fragile, velvetlike lining called a
mucous membrane. Frequently, when a woman
has been raped, the cervical canal and vaginal
lips are red and inflamed. In some cases, es-

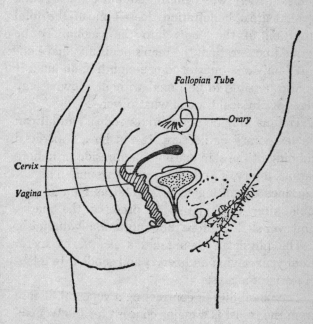

Internal Female Sex Organs

pecially in children, the lining of the canal turns inside out (cervical eversion).

Because you are naturally tense and upset, the insertion of the speculum may be extremely uncomfortable and often painful. Try taking slow, deep breaths to help relax your muscles while being examined. Specula come in different sizes and a special one is used for children and young women. A smaller speculum also can be used if you are very nervous.

The medical examination for rape also determines if there was penetration and trauma of the genital area. Penetration doesn't mean the total insertion of the penis into the vagina. To be termed penetration, the man's penis may have entered only one-quarter to one-eighth of an inch. It is also possible to be raped without showing any signs of physical trauma whatsoever.

Trauma may be any mark or redness and it can be temporary or fleeting. It can be a superficial rubbing of the skin causing an abrasion or a more serious injury, a knife or gunshot wound. The importance of getting to a hospital as soon as possible after the rape is to preserve the marks, however slight, before they substantially diminish.

The physician then takes a sample of sperm from your vagina and cervix and sends it to a laboratory for analysis.

The possibility of contracting a venereal disease from the rapist is a major concern for the woman. The doctor performs tests for gonorrhea and syphilis as part of the examination, but these tests tell you only whether you had the disease *at the time of the rape.* The tests won't determine whether or not you will later contract it from the rapist. The symptoms of venereal disease do not appear immediately after genital contact with an infected person. So women frequently show no outward symptoms of VD and don't realize they've caught it. It takes about one week after intercourse for the gonorrhea test to turn positive; three to four weeks for the syphilis test, so it's necessary to return to the doctor one week after the medical examination to test for gonorrhea and then six weeks later to test for syphilis.

THE EXAMINATION AND TEST FOR GONORRHEA

Most hospitals test for venereal disease as a standard procedure during the medical examination. With the speculum in place, the doctor inserts a cotton swab about one-half inch into the cervical canal and takes a small sample of the discharge.

There are two currently used methods for testing gonorrhea: the smear or gram stain and the culture. No acceptable blood test exists. Almost 65% of women who are infected with gonorrhea have negative results from the gram stain so it's useless for women. Instead, the doctor should take the discharge from the cotton swab and place it on a specially prepared culture plate. The culture plate is a round, shallow dish that contains a brown, jellylike substance. This jelly (culture medium) filters out all bacteria except the germs which cause gonorrhea. The plate is then put into an incubator, a closed container which keeps a constant temperature of 98 degrees. Once inside the incubator, the germs begin to multiply and grow. After 48 hours, clumps or colonies of the coffee-bean shaped germs appear on the surface of the plate.

Unless you had gonorrhea prior to being raped, it takes one week before the disease-causing germs are detectible in the culture test. So you must return to the doctor for further testing.

If the rapist forced you to have oral or anal intercourse, a culture is also taken from these areas. These procedures take only a few minutes and aren't painful.

THE TEST FOR SYPHILIS

The test for syphilis is a simple blood test called VDRL, developed at the Venereal Disease Research Laboratories in Atlanta. This is a routine blood test given to couples who apply for a marriage license, pregnant women, people donating blood and anyone who joins the armed forces.

The test works by detecting "antibodies" in the blood sample taken from your arm. When the germs which cause syphilis have been in your bloodstream for about three to four weeks, your body produces a specific chemical or antibody which attaches itself to the germs and attempts to destroy them.

Since antibodies aren't produced until several weeks after the time you are infected, you must return at least four to six weeks after the rape occurred.

TREATMENT FOR VENEREAL DISEASE

Providing you have no allergy to penicillin, you generally will receive 4.8 million units of procaine penicillin G, given in two injections (one in each buttock). The idea is to inject a massive amount of the antibiotic into the bloodstream. Procaine penicillin G is a fast-acting penicillin which is distributed throughout the body for 12 hours, after which the amount in the bloodstream drops and disappears completely within 24 hours. The procaine in the penicillin is a local anesthetic that helps to reduce the pain of such a large injection. In addition to the injections, you may be given one gram of probenecid taken by mouth 30 minutes before the injections. Probenecid helps the bloodstream absorb penicillin at a faster rate.

The injections may be somewhat uncomfortable but they aren't painful. The muscles of the buttocks may be sore for several days after treatment. Rubbing or massaging the area helps reduce the soreness.

Some hospitals are now administering 3.5 grams

of ampicillin (oral penicillin) in place of these injections.

SIDE EFFECTS OF PENICILLIN

Unless you're allergic to the drug, penicillin is one of the safest antibiotics used today. However, if you have a previous history of a reaction or if you have a severe allergy such as asthma, tell the doctor right away.

Sometimes women develop an itching and discharge from the vagina. This disappears within a few days. Another common type of reaction to penicillin is a "delayed" reaction. It usually appears as a skin rash 7–14 days after the drug is taken. Some women have a low-grade fever and feel sick to their stomachs. This reaction is usually harmless and disappears in several days. However, if you develop any of these symptoms, report it to the doctor.

If you are allergic to penicillin, a host of other antibiotics are available to treat venereal disease effectively.

TETRACYCLINE

Tetracycline is an alternative drug given to people who are allergic to penicillin. It is usually taken by mouth (0.5 gm) every six hours for no less than 12 days. Tetracycline is given orally because an injection is very painful. Unlike penicillin, which is absorbed directly into the bloodstream, tetracycline is absorbed from the stomach and small intestine and then distributed to the rest of the body. Common side effects of tetracycline are nausea, heartburn, vomiting and diarrhea. These symptoms are harmless and will disappear after the second or third pill.

Take this drug on an empty stomach to lessen the side effects and don't eat for one hour. If you forget to take a pill, take it just as soon as you remember, even if you have to take two at a time.

Tetracycline is a relatively safe drug but is hazardous to pregnant women. It can damage the liver and may be fatal. The drug also affects the fetus, discoloring the teeth and producing abnormalities in the bones. Pregnant women must not take tetracycline.

Other drugs used to treat venereal disease:

Spectinomycin—2 to 4 gm. injected into the buttocks.

Cephaloridine—2 gm. daily, injected into the buttocks for two consecutive days.

Doxycycline or minocycline—100 mg. capsule, twice a day for two days.

PREGNANCY

If you weren't using a contraceptive (birth-control pill, IUD) at the time of the rape, the doctor may give you diethylstilbesterol (DES), commonly known as the morning-after pill. There is a serious possibility of your becoming pregnant if the rape occurred between 10 and 18 days before the start of your menstrual period.

DES is an artificial estrogen (hormone) which, when given within 24 to 36 hours after intercourse, inhibits ovulation. The drug creates a chemical barrier which affects the lining of the uterus, making it impervious to a fertilized egg. However, the morning-after pill is highly controversial and has been linked to producing cancer in female children, so you may prefer to wait and have a menstrual extraction. Menstrual extraction is a procedure still under observation and research so be sure to ask a doctor you trust for his or her opinion of this option.

DES is given in small doses (25 mg.), two pills a day for five days and you must begin taking them within 72 hours after the rape. DES prevents you from becoming pregnant but does not affect an already existing fetus.

SIDE EFFECTS OF STILBESTEROL

DES causes extreme nausea and vomiting which is intensified when the drug is taken on an empty stomach. Make sure you eat something before taking this drug. It is also common for your breasts to become tender and for your menstrual period to be up to one week late. Some women also complain of vaginal spotting and headaches. The side effects generally diminish each day you take the pills and your menstrual period returns to normal once the drug is out of your system.

AN IMPORTANT NOTE ON THE MORNING-AFTER PILL

DES was discovered in the 1930s. During the '40s and '50s, many doctors believed that it should be prescribed to women who had histories of miscarriages and who wanted to avoid another. After more than a decade of use and thousands of prescriptions, it was discovered that the drug had no effect whatsoever on repeated miscarriages.

But in the 1960s, the girls born to women who had been given the drug began to go through puberty. Some of them developed a cancer called adencarcinoma of the vagina. In 1973 a major drive was started in the cities to alert all women between 20 and 30 to ask their mothers if they were given DES during their pregnancy. If your mother is not aware of taking this drug, call her family doctor or gynecologist. It should be noted on the chart.

If your mother did take DES during her pregnancy, you must be examined for vaginal cancer every six months for the rest of your life.

So far, the incidence of vaginal cancer is low, only 100 cases out of several thousand, with only a total of 400 women found to have it, but the threat is prevalent enough to warrant concern.

FOLLOW-UP EXAMINATIONS

You must return to the doctor one week after the medical examination to have a culture test for gonorrhea and at least six weeks afterwards for a syphilis blood test. Remember, if you caught venereal disease from the rapist, you won't be cured with the penicillin you received during the examination. It takes time for the disease-causing germs to incubate in your body before they can be combated by the penicillin.

Psychological Scars

Rape is a violent physical crime but the aftereffects are often harrowing. A woman who has been raped can't be expected to return to normal immediately. She sees the world from a perspective clouded by fear, guilt, embarrassment and/or anger. Her feelings can be intensified by those people closest to her: family, friends, lovers, husbands who don't understand and don't know how to cope with the fact that she has been raped. Especially if she is a young woman, perhaps a teenager, her parents may have trouble believing that she was in no way responsible for being raped.

"I'd like, I'd really like to believe my Judy didn't ask for this. But, honestly, those short skirts she wears . . . and no bra . . . I hate myself for thinking this, but isn't that kind of an invitation?"

A New England rape victim's father

YOUR MAN

A man's reaction to his wife's or lover's rape is almost always a complex and changing one. His feelings are certain to be intense but they are also likely to be conflicting.

Probably the first and most universal reflex is anger. Many men feel the desire to walk the street in search of their wives' rapists. They think about killing the man, think about it in a way that they have never considered such an action before. Some even try to locate the attacker and search for days in the neighborhood of the rape for a man more or less fitting the description of the rapist.

But the emotions that form the basis of this anger are those that become more important as time goes on. Anger and the wish for revenge are simply the symptoms of a man's feelings. And those undercurrents can vary widely.

"I wanted to kill that bastard. I wanted to destroy him for what he'd done to me."

Some men feel personally attacked. They think of their wives as part of themselves, or their property, and so they think of the rape as one man's attack on another man's domain. There is in these men a confusion of feeling surrounding their ideas concerning women. They sometimes betray themselves as thinking, basically, that rape has significance only to them, or at least most directly

to them. Their wives are simply the victims and
vehicles of the insult.

Obviously any woman who finds herself with a
lover or husband who, rather than being sympathetic and helpful, is vengeful and insulted will
certainly feel distant from him. And this is a difficult time to close the impending chasm between
the two of you.

Some men react to a rape with disgust. They
simply are repulsed by the thought, the act, the
very physical intimacy of it. Some find their wives
have difficulty approaching sex, have a hard time
regaining the pattern of their relationships with
men. And this of course has its effect on your sex
life. You may be injured, either physically or emo-
tionally or both, to the point where sex is simply
impossible for a time. You'll be confused by that
reaction. But more confusing to many women is
the disgust with which they are treated by their
lovers. As though they had been permanently
soiled by the attack. As though the victim were
responsible for complicity in the rape.

Perhaps the most painful reaction is disinterest.
Some men seem to feel that rape is little more
than a sexual event, not terribly significant and
upsetting only to a woman who exaggerates her
own importance.

*"I told her to forget it. It was over, she was all
right. So what's the big deal? I mean, he didn't
beat her. Then she wanted to call the police.
Jesus, cops, courtrooms, going over and over it. I*

*couldn't believe what she wanted to get us into.
So I told her to forget it. Just forget the whole
thing and let it go. Can you believe she wouldn't
listen to me? Can you believe she went through
the whole thing, two and a half years, to convict
some guy for rape?"*

Most men react with sympathy and kindness to
the rape of their wives. They are angry for a
while, feel attacked themselves and then come to
understand the real pain and the actual ordeal.
Most men try to help even though they don't really understand what it is to be raped. But they understand your suffering and do the best they can
to lessen it.

Be ready to help him help you. Face whatever
emotions you feel by talking about them openly.
Discuss your feelings about sex—even with him—as
clearly as you can. Try to understand that he has
a right to his anger. Discuss it with him and think
about the fact that the rape has damaged him too.
The trauma, the brutality, the injustice and the
guilt of the rape are bound to change your love.
Accept that as soon as you can, and start taking
the steps together, to grow out of it.

HELP

Both the rape victim and her family need fol-
low-up counseling to talk about their feelings before they fester and become destructive. If you
are fortunate enough to have a rape crisis center

in your area, this service will be easier for you to receive. The crisis centers are specifically geared toward the needs of the rape victim. There are special telephone hot lines available for a woman to talk about her rape no matter how long ago it occurred. If you wish, the center will refer you to an individual counselor or you can attend rap groups. These groups give you the opportunity to share your experiences with other women who are going through the same difficulties in adjusting. Many centers have specific groups for adults, adolescents and for the parents of children who have been raped. In addition, some centers will provide individual counseling to husbands, parents and relatives.

MOAR

The first group of Men Organized Against Rape (MOAR) was formed in Philadelphia and the outlying suburbs. MOAR's intention is to shatter the specifically male-oriented myths of rape and to talk with the victim's male friends, relatives or lovers at special weekend rap sessions held at Presbyterian Hospital. The men also speak with male callers on a telephone hot line.

Surprisingly, the MOAR sometimes receives calls from rapists or potential rapists who are concerned about their abnormal impulses and want help. They don't want to talk to women; they want to tell another man. If a greater number of active MOAR groups can be founded throughout the United States, countless rapes may be prevented. There are some ways in which only a man can help. The potential of future MOAR groups is tremendous.

The Formal Statement

The procedure varies from city to city and from suburb to suburb, but you generally have to return to the police station to give a formal statement. Depending on the time of the rape and your physical condition, you may be asked to return immediately or the following day. The statement is usually given before a detective and a police officer, who may or may not be women. As recently as three years ago, rape victims were questioned only by men, but due to the pressure of today's rape crisis centers, the situation is changing. New York City, Detroit, Miami, Washington, D.C., Chicago and many other large metropolitan areas now have women detectives on the force to handle the rape interviews.

The purpose of the formal statement is to cover every possible detail of the rape. The police interviewer refers to the initial report filed by the policeman who answered your call for help and asks you to go into even greater detail about what happened. The police want to make certain that your statement hasn't changed and want you to answer more questions about the rapist's mode of operation (MO). You may feel as though you are being badgered and doubted. The police often do this purposely to verify that the rape happened just the way you described it to the first policeman. Also they want to find out any information you might have missed or forgotten. Be frank and thorough; tell them everything no matter how unimportant it may seem to you.

During the interview, the detective probably will ask you to look at pictures of various men to see if the man who attacked you is among them. If you don't recognize him from the "mug shots," you may be asked to describe the man to a police artist who puts together a composite drawing which is distributed to police officers throughout the city.

In some cities the police may ask you to take a lie detector test. You don't have to take this test if you don't want to. This is a personal choice and the police have no right to insist. Whether or not you take it doesn't mean a thing to you. The fact that you refused to take the test isn't admissible in a court of law and if you do take it, and the results are unfavorable, they can be excluded in the trial.

If the police have one or several suspects, you'll be asked to identify the assailant in person at a line-up. Several men file into a room as you stand unseen behind a one-way glass. A police officer and an attorney for the suspect will be present. If a man looks familiar to you, tell the officer to have him say those words or phrases which the rapist said to you. (All the other line-up members then also must be asked to speak the same words in the same manner.) If you positively identify him as the one who attacked you, a form is filled out in order to get a warrant. Then you and the police officer go to the prosecutor's office where a warrant is issued for the man's arrest on the charge of rape. Then you'll probably go to the clerks office and swear that the charges are true. After this is done, you are free to go home.

If your attacker is not among the suspects in the line-up, you may be asked to return at a later date to view other line-ups. If you are threatened or if you have any reason to believe that the man will return and hurt you, you can ask for police protection.

"When I got home after the police questioning, the phone rang. I was still dazed, a little shaky and my stomach was funny. They'd (the police) told me that they'd circle the area around my house for a while but no one had shown up yet. I'm not sure how long, but I think I let it ring forever. When I picked it up it was him. I knew it was him before he said what he did. He said, 'I know you told them (the police); you'd better drop charges; if you don't drop the charges I'm coming back. I'll kill you and I'll kill your daughter, too. I mean it, God, I mean it.' He meant it. He came the next night and beat me with a bent-up tin can. I was in the hospital for three days. God, he meant it."

A 47-year-old Delaware rape victim

The only people who have the right to ask you questions about the rape are the policemen who initially came to your home or answered your call and the detective assigned to your case. You don't have to make a statement to any other police officer.

THE PRETRIAL OR PRELIMINARY HEARING

Before the preliminary hearing, you're questioned by a Deputy District Attorney who goes over the statements you gave to the police and to the doctor during the medical examination. The Deputy D.A. also asks you the type of questions that you can expect the defense attorney (suspect's attorney) to ask during a trial. Usually within three days to two weeks after the incident the detective notifies you of the date and time of the preliminary hearing.

The purpose of this hearing is to determine if there is enough evidence to bring your case into court. The Deputy D.A. recounts the details of the rape. Then you're questioned by the rapist's attorney, who goes over your testimony inch by inch to try and find some weakness that he can use to his client's advantage. At this time, the defense attorney usually asks you questions about your private life. He is trying to do all he can to scare you out of proceeding with the case and to pressure you to drop the charges. You can expect questions like: Do you have a boyfriend and are you intimate with him? Do you sleep with him and how often? When did you last have intercourse? When was the first time you had intercourse? Are you married and do you see other men?

Remember, you are being pressured to drop the charges and the defense attorney is trying to frighten you by making you feel as though you have more to lose than the rapist. Keep your head together and don't let him frighten you.

Be honest with him; he can always investigate the truth of your story. Remember, too, that he may be trying to ascertain your weak points. The questions you don't answer now, or hedge about, are the ones he'll emphasize in court when you *must* answer.

PLEA BARGAINING

Plea bargaining takes place between your lawyer (prosecution) and the defense lawyer. This is a private matter between the lawyers and you aren't present to see what actually goes on. The rapist's attorney tries to get your attorney to accept a lesser charge than rape. If you were threatened with a weapon, the defense may ask that the charge be assault instead of rape. This arrangement is called *copping a plea* and is partially responsible for the scarcity of rape trials. Under this deal the rapist pleads guilty to a charge other than rape and the case never has to go to trial. The rapist pleads guilty to assault, for example, and is then sentenced by the judge. So if you decide to accept a lesser charge, you won't have to testify in a court trial. That idea is, of course, attractive. The Deputy D.A. approaches you with the offer of plea bargaining and may tell you that it's an easier solution for you than going through the rigors of a trial. Easier, yes. More just, no. Remember, if you were raped, the man you are prosecuting is a rapist and *the charge is rape*. If you don't prosecute, you're helping to put this rapist back on the streets.

The Trial

Once you've decided to prosecute the rapist, you've got a long wait. Some time ten months to two years after the rape, the District Attorney's office serves you with a subpoena requiring you to appear in court and testify. The courts have a long backlog of cases and your case is added to the end of the list. Though you may want to get it over with, courts are always overcrowded; you'll have to wait.

The rapist's attorney may attempt to use this wait to his own advantage. He may try to stall the trial for as long as he possibly can. This postponement is called a "continuance" and the court generally allows the attorney several continuances. From the defense attorney's viewpoint, the longer the delay, the better the chances that you'll give up the case. The idea is that a woman who has been raped one year ago will not press charges because she'd rather the rape be over and forgotten. Elapsed time always cushions the immediate effects of her rape. One or two years later the victim has ceased viewing herself as a "victim," her bitterness has diminished and she has no desire to relive the agonizing details of her rape in a courtroom. Moreover, the probability that the details of the incident will become hazy in the victim's mind grows as time passes. You are questioned at the trial as if the rape occurred yesterday, not one or two years before. You're expected to reveal and relive every aspect of the rape. The defense attorney is hoping that you won't testify, or can't testify effectively, so you'll drop the charges.

If you do decide to continue with the trial, you'll find that the rapist has a legal right either to a trial by jury or a trial with only a judge. He often opts for the jury, since it puts you in the uncomfortable position of telling the embarrassing details in front of an audience. Also, the rapist has a better chance of receiving a verdict of not guilty when he's tried by a jury. Persons on a jury aren't always aware of the intricacies of the law and the possible legal bulldozing and whitewashing attempts of the defense attorney. They are apt to be shocked by the woman's past life (if it is allowed to be brought up) and are prone to judge her credibility on the basis of her personal history.

On the other hand, a judge has tried rape cases before. He knows exactly what the rapist's lawyer is trying to do and isn't fooled by it. It's therefore no surprise when the rapist chooses a jury.

The burden of accusation rests with you and the Assistant District Attorney (prosecution). You must prove, beyond a reasonable doubt, that this man is guilty of rape. He doesn't have to prove anything, in fact, he doesn't even have to take the stand if he so desires. Often he won't say one word throughout the entire trial. He doesn't have to.

CHOOSING A JURY

The following is taken from a Transcript of Notes of Testimony from a Pennsylvania trial for rape in 1970 and concerns the questions asked to prospective jurors by the defense attorney (for the rapist). The defense begins by asking if anyone knows any of the persons involved in this case; the attorneys, defendant (accused), the rape victim, or any other witnesses. He then asks:

"Is there anyone here who feels that the defendant would have to testify on his own behalf before you could find him not guilty of the charge? Is there anyone who feels the defendant would have to testify on his own behalf before you could find him not guilty?

"I assume by the fact that there is no response that nobody would consider it adverse to the defendant if he did not take the stand in this case."

Since this case involved the rape of a 16-year-old girl, the defense attorney also asks if there is any member on the panel who has teenage daughters. If so, they might be prejudiced toward the young victim.

Attorneys also often ask if anyone on the panel has had a close friend or relative who was raped. This too might prejudice the jury, against the rapist.

THE CASE

Once the jury is chosen, the rape victim is sworn in and questioned by her attorney (direct examination). She is taken through the incidents leading up to the rape, the rape itself and those events that followed. In this particular case a 16-year-old girl was raped by a man who was supposed to be giving her driving lessons. She is questioned by her own attorney.

Q. What happened then?

A. Then he stopped the car and turned out the lights. And he tried to kiss me, and I pulled away, and I told him to take me home; and he grabbed me by the neck and pulled me over toward him.

Q. And what was the state of your emotions at this time?

A. I was crying. I told him to take me home.

Q. And how many times did you tell him to take you home, do you recall?

A. A couple of times.

Q. What did he say, if anything?

A. He said to get into the back of the car or else I would never get home.

The attorney continues to ask her about every aspect of the rape . . . when she told her parents, what happened at the hospital, what she did immediately afterwards, how she resisted, how she felt at the time, etc. When he completes his questioning, the defense attorney takes over. Up until this time the rape victim is allowed to tell her story uninterrupted. One of the functions of the defense attorney is to discredit the witness by whatever means he or she can. By concentrating on the victim instead of the accused, the attorney shifts the focus away from his client and puts the pressure on the rape victim.

If you are asked a question which you don't understand, take your time and ask the lawyer to repeat it. If you are asked a question that you think has no bearing in the case, pause for a moment and give the Assistant D.A. time to object. If he or she doesn't object, ask the judge if you must answer the question and if the judge says yes, then answer.

Most states allow a defense attorney to question a woman in the courtroom about her past sexual history. Rape victims have often lost their cases because a lawyer has done a fine job of casting aspersions regarding the promiscuity of the women. Ironically, the rapist's past history is barred from the court, since it is his constitutional right to be tried for only one case at a time and previous arrests or convictions may not be mentioned. Unless you live in Iowa or California you can expect to be asked questions about your private life. These states recently changed the law to prohibit defense attorneys from probing into a woman's prior sexual experiences. There are also some individual judges who refuse to admit this kind of inquiry

Since this book first was published, some changes have taken place in Pennsylvania. Now, a victim's past sexual history can be brought up only (1) if she had prior sex with the defendant; and (2), the question of consent is at issue. In fact, there has been an increase in the number of rapes actually reported because of the rule changes concerning the victim's prior sexual conduct. This willingness to report rape also may be due to the improvement in the criminal justice system's handling of rape victims, an impact of the women's movement.

The defense attorney attempts to discredit your testimony regardless of your age. During her cross-examination, the 16-year-old Pennsylvania girl was asked:

Q. How long were you screaming?

A. A couple of seconds.

Q. A couple of seconds?

A. Yes, I was screaming. Then I just kept crying.

Q. You previously testified that you were screaming for ten minutes, at the preliminary hearing.

A. I don't know. (The preliminary hearing took place over one year before the trial while the girl was 16-years-old.)

Q. Did Mr. X. have an erection?

A. I don't know.

Q. Do you know what an erection is?

A. No.

Q. Did you ever have intercourse before?

With that, the Assistant District Attorney objected and it was sustained.

The defense attorney continued to batter away at the credibility of the teenager, asking her questions about one aspect of the rape then quickly changing to another. After a while she was shaken and confused.

Q. I asked you previously if Mr. X. had an erection at the time of this alleged rape, and as I recall, your answer was that you did not know what an erection was. Is that what your testimony is?

A. I wasn't sure what you meant.

Q. Do you know what I mean now?

A. Yes.

Q. How do you know now? What have I said different?

A. You said he—

Q. Have you spoken with somebody? Have you spoken with the District Attorney about that question?

A. No.

Q. What is an erection?

A. When a—when a man—

Defense Attorney: Again let the record indicate a pause.

Q. Come on Ms. A., you know what an erection is, don't you?

A. Yes, but I don't know how to explain it.

Q. Why didn't you answer my question when I asked you this morning as to what an erection was?

A. Cause I wasn't sure.

Q. You didn't say that, did you? You said you didn't know what an erection was. You didn't say you weren't sure. You in fact have knowledge from previous experience what an erection is.

District Attorney: Objection, Your Honor.

Court: Objection sustained.

There is almost no limit to the ploys some defense attorneys use to make the victim appear a harlot. This courtroom strategy of discrediting the victim's sexual mores is condoned in the majority of our cities. The legal system encourages defense attorneys to discredit what may be the only witness, the victim, and humiliate her, or it forces her to drop the charges, and in the end allows the jury to release her rapist.

The conviction rate for rapists is deplorable. This isn't surprising since our court system discourages successful prosecution, turning the victim into a defendant.

And so the trial proceeds, with a parade of witnesses testifying, being examined and cross-examined. You're often required to leave the courtroom and stand outside, so you won't be within hearing range of the witnesses' answers, for fear that you might change your story based on the testimony of another. However, after you are no longer needed to testify, you can remain in the courtroom for the rest of the trial.

When all the details have been covered to the satisfaction of both lawyers, the defense attorney addresses the jury in what is known as a summation. This final effort to convince the jury of the innocence of the rapist stresses the importance of having a reasonable doubt. He or she will take the case step by step and point by point.

"1. The defendant comes before you cloaked in a mantel of innocence. This defendant, like every defendant who comes before a jury in a criminal court, is presumed to be innocent and this presumption of innocence remains with him not only at the inception of the trial but through the course of the proceedings, and until such time as you, the jury, by a consideration of all the evidence . . . conclude that the defendant is guilty of the offense charges beyond a reasonable doubt.

3. "The defendant does not have any burden of proving or disproving anything in this trial.

8. "If it has been shown to you beyond a reasonable doubt that this defendant did have sexual intercourse with the prosecuting witness, then your next inquiry will be whether the defendant accomplished this by the use of force of sufficient intensity to make the carnal knowledge against her will and without her consent. If there was no force, or if consent was given, then even though there may have been carnal knowledge, the defendant would not be guilty of rape. In such a

case, you would find him guilty of the lesser offense of fornication which is defined as unlawful sexual intercourse, but the act was consented to by the female.

14. "Now, the credibility of the witnesses is entirely for you to believe. The Court has nothing to say as to whom you will believe, or what weight you will give the testimony of any witnesses. The appearance and demeanor of a witness are essential elements of consideration in determining whether he has spoken the truth. All of the usual indicia of truthfulness which you have learned to respect in the affairs of everyday life will come to your aid in this respect. A spontaneous gesture, a lift of the eyebrow, a shrug of a shoulder, an intonation of voice, a flash of the eye, or the facial expression employed are a few of the vital and influential indicia of credibility which you may consider.

20. "Ladies and Gentlemen, you as members of the jury must consider and weigh the testimony given as to the bad reputation for morality and chastity of the prosecuting witness, Ms. A., in consideration with all the other testimony of Ms. A., in determining the credibility of her testimony.

"Rape is a crime which ordinarily is not committed in the presence of witnesses. For this reason the testimony of the prosecuting witness, Ms. A., and her credibility must be scrutinized by you and considered most carefully. You should make scrutiny particularly with a view toward determining whether there was intercourse without consent. Did her story have a ring of truth?

"One of the most important tests of a woman's sincerity in this type of action is the question of whether she cried aloud, whether she struggled or complained at the first opportunity, whether she brought about a prosecution of the defendant without inexcusable delay; was it a prompt outcry and was her complaint brought promptly?"

The jury deliberates and ultimately reaches a verdict. However, their final decision is not always dependent upon the fact that you were raped and that this is the man who raped you. Ironically, the verdict rests with you: your manner, your appearance, often your past life and your credibility. You are on trial.

SENTENCING

In the case of the 17-year-old girl, the jury reached a unanimous verdict of guilty. The final decision was somewhat surprising, considering the tactics used by the defense attorney to badger, discredit and pressure the victim.

Throughout the trial, which lasted five days, the defendant never took the stand, never uttered a word. After the verdict was given, the judge addressed the accused.

The Court: I am sure you will want to file a motion in the next ten days or so.

Defense Attorney: Your Honor, the defendant

at this time indicates to me he would prefer to be sentenced at this time.

The Court: With regard to this matter, you have the right to file appropriate motions for a new trial and motion for arrest of judgment which the court would hear, and then you have a right to appeal from that to a Superior and Appellate court.

Defendant: I don't want to appeal.

The Court: Well, I suggest that you do this. You discuss this with your lawyer, and then tell me on Monday and I will confer sentencing then.

Defendent: Your Honor, I'd sooner you sentence me now, cause I don't want to come back here Monday. I don't want the aggravation.

The Court: I know you are upset, sir.

Defendant: That's all right. I want to get it over with. This thing has been going on for a year. I have had to live with this for a year.

The Court: Talk with your lawyer, if you don't want to file a motion, I will sentence on Monday.

Defendant: I don't want no motion, I don't want no appeal. There's too much money been spent now. My people's old. There's almost eight thousand dollars went to lawyers, detectives in this case.

Defense Attorney: For the record, I think it should be indicated it is not in this case, Your Honor, it's other cases.

The Court: I'm going to defer sentencing in this matter at least until Monday morning.

Defendant: I still ask you to sentence me.

The Court: I know you are upset, sir, I can appreciate that.

Defendant: I'm not upset. I'm asking you to sentence me now.

The Court: The court is going to defer sentencing to give your counsel the opportunity to file motions within the appropriate time. Thank you.

The maximum penalty for rape in Pennsylvania is 10–20 years. This means that if the defendant receives the maximum, he will be eligible for parole in ten years. In at least ten states the maximum penalty for rape is death or life imprisonment. Clearly, these are long sentences. Many lawmakers feel that the conviction rates for the crime will increase if the penalty for it is reduced to a fewer number of years. They reason that juries are reluctant to convict in light of the gravity of the minimum sentence. And this is almost certainly the case. Considering the legal requirement of the court in its sentencing, it is only natural for a jury to give greater weight to its doubts in light of longer and more severe penalties upon conviction. In short, they acquit more readily as a result of their reluctance to convict if even the slightest doubt can be entertained.

The solution here is far from a simple one. Clearly, the banning of any reference to a woman's past sexual conduct would improve the objective consideration of the case by jurors. But as long as convicted rapists are guaranteed long sentences and little hope of counseling and rehabilitation, juries will continue to consider very heavily any doubts as to guilt that a defense attorney can raise. The line between reasonable and unreasonable doubt is a fine one. And it must be carefully considered by juries. But, the sexual experience of the victim should not enter into the balance. It is, simply enough, not the victim who is on trial.

The Child Victim

"What kind of animal would rape a nine-year-old child?"

Mother of a New Jersey rape victim

Rape doesn't discriminate according to age. In fact, the majority of rape victims studied by Amir were 10 to 19 years old and national statistics have noted rape victims as young as six months. In July of 1974 a Philadelphia man was arrested for raping a 22-month-old infant. He was babysitting for the child while her mother was shopping. The infant later died.

Who would rape a child? According to Amir's findings they are generally older men, middle-aged and upward. They are usually men who rape only children, not older women. Often they are strangers but sometimes they are friends of the child's parents, neighbors or even relatives. The child often has no idea of what has happened to her. What does a three-year-old know about rape? How do you begin to explain rape—or forced sexual intercourse—to a nine-year-old? How do you as a parent or guardian make sense out of it yourself?

If the child is older, she may think that her friends and relatives are ashamed of her or that they don't believe her. Then again, she might simply be terribly afraid.

It was the fear of having the man return which stopped me from telling my parents that I was raped. I was 10 years old, riding my bike home from school, when a car pulled alongside and the driver motioned for me to stop. I did. Like every child, I had been properly versed in the eleventh commandment for children, "Thou shalt not trust strange men," but he seemed nice enough. He was a man older than my father. He got out of the car and asked me for directions, then grabbed my arm and pulled me into the car. I had no idea what happened or what rape was.

He said that if I told anyone he would come back and kill my family. I remember walking home crying, hurt, bleeding, my school uniform torn. When my mother asked me what happened, I told her I had fallen from my bike.

It took me 13 years to finally tell her. We spent hours holding each other, crying. She cried for her 10-year-old daughter. I cried for a 13-year-old secret that didn't have to be a secret anymore.

A young child doesn't understand rape and will react in the same way that you, as a parent, react. If you show anger toward the rapist in front of your child, she may think you are angry with her. Because she doesn't have any feelings or emotions of her own specifically about rape, she mirrors yours.

If the child is very young, it isn't necessary for you to go into detail about what happened. It's more important for you to be calm and explain that you are both going to see the doctor because she may be hurt and the doctor is going to look at her, etc. Use your own words and be gentle. The child needs your love and support, so leave your anger at home. Don't force her to talk about what happened and on the other hand, don't recoil when she wants to tell you. She will probably be confused and bewildered and she'll look to you for help.

Once the hospital ordeal is over, have her continue her normal activities as soon as possible. Don't dwell on the rape. She needs to be a child again. Do your best not to make it seem that the rape has made a difference to you. Remember children take everything you say and apply it to themselves. It's normal for you as a parent to feel guilty, as though you were in some way responsible. You feel you should have done something to prevent it. But you weren't responsible. There is no logical way to explain the rape of a child, just as there is often no way to account for any rape, regardless of the victim's age.

The healthiest thing for you to do is to take the anger you're feeling and direct it toward finding the man who raped your child. Do all you can to help the police find him and then prosecute.

The court is tremendously sympathetic in handling the trial of a child rape victim. The trial is not the traumatic experience that an adult woman undergoes. Your daughter may be asked to identify the man and answer one or two questions about what happened. She will then leave the courtroom.

The teenage victim has a different set of problems after she is raped. She may feel guilty, embarrassed and ashamed. She may not tell you for fear that you will feel that she in some way provoked the attack. There is a possibility that she may not be believed, that you will doubt her.

Don't spend time beating your chest saying "how could this happen to me?" Don't feel sorry for yourself. You're not the one who was raped, your daughter was. Think about the pain she's going through. She needs you desperately. Sometimes we feel so hurt that we take our anger out on the person who needs us most. So what if she shouldn't have been walking the streets at night, or perhaps you disagree with the way she dresses. That doesn't matter now. You can spend the rest of your life saying "if only she . . ." and it won't mean a thing. It isn't easy for you as a parent to see your child so frightened and upset. Of course it's painful but your daughter comes first.

8
The Rape
Crisis Center

STARTING A RAPE CRISIS CENTER

The following outline is the basis on which rape crisis centers are founded. Several publications put out by rape crisis centers are listed that deal specifically and extensively with every aspect of establishing a center in your city or town.

THE LOCATION OF THE CENTER

Before you seriously consider where to house your center, keep in mind that rent for office space is high. You'll be put in the position of raising money just to keep up with your rent. Ask churches, YWCA's, universities, hospitals and civic organizations to donate space. One problem: if such groups do offer space, they may limit your function and restrict your freedom as a rape crisis center. Go over all the possibilities before you decide.

Consider also the physical location of your center. You want to be in the vicinity of those institutions (hospital, police department, courts) with which you will have contact. Choose a safe area since your volunteers may be in and out at all hours.

THE POST OFFICE BOX NUMBER

Once you find a place you are going to need a way to be reached. The P.O. box number is the only way to accomplish this. Never use a woman's name or home address for correspondence. You want to remain personally anonymous in case of crank calls or press hounds, and the P.O. box number will identify you as an organized group instead of just one person.

INCORPORATE

There are specific laws in most states which apply to incorporating non-profit groups. They will be geared to the functions of your particular group. The details are incredibly complicated so you will need to get a lawyer. If you can't afford an attorney, you can ask a law firm in your town to donate their services or get in touch with the Lawyers Reference Agency in your area. They will handle the matter for a minimal charge (usually based on the ability to pay).

Incorporating your rape crisis center is worth the hassles of a lawyer. In fact, it's necessary. When your group incorporates, no one person is liable to be sued for debts. The group as a whole is still liable for any debts but one individual member cannot be held. Otherwise, should you run into financial debt, your president or f~under will be personally liable.

In addition, the group is legally protected

should your founder leave. Another reason for incorporating is to more easily achieve a tax-exempt status.

THE HOW-TO'S OF
TAX EXEMPTION

The Internal Revenue Service offers a special publication dealing with ways to attain a tax-exempt status. Write the IRS, 10th and Pennsylvania Aves., Washington, D.C. Ask for pamphlet #557.

Once you gain a tax-exempt status, you don't have to pay any taxes, including sales tax, and you are eligible for federal funds and grants from private foundations. Also, as a tax-exempt organization, you enable a contributor to write off his donation as a tax deduction.

A drawback of your tax-exempt status is that you are prohibited from engaging in political lobbying or any political activity. The IRS is extremely vigilant in monitoring tax-exempt groups, so this is one promise you have to keep. If the IRS finds evidence of your political activity, your group will lose its tax-exempt status and you will be forced to pay back taxes.

In order to apply for this status you will need the help of a lawyer. The procedures and applications for incorporating and establishing your center as a tax-exempt organization will take months to accomplish, so if you want to apply, do it as soon as you can.

HOT LINE

The hot line is a crucial part of your operation as a rape crisis center since your primary function will be counseling rape victims and their families. If you are thinking about having a 24-hour hot line, you must be able to have enough volunteers willing to staff the phones. You should expect your first few months to be slow but the number of calls will build up gradually with press exposure as women become aware of the center's existence.

If you initially lack the staff members necessary to operate a 24-hour hot line, you might consider having at least some of your telephone hours during regular business hours since you will frequently have to call other agencies (abortion, medical and legal counseling). But remember that most rapes occur after dark; you want your line available when it's most needed.

FUNCTIONS OF A RAPE CRISIS CENTER:

1. Provide the woman with immediate information concerning the medical examination, police questioning and court procedures.
2. Accompany her to the hospital, police or courts if she wishes.
3. Offer rap groups and/or refer women to individual counselors.
4. Work for changes in police and hospital handling and treatment of rape victims.

5. Keep the media informed of the changes and the need for change.
6. Have volunteers speak on the topic of rape in women's clubs, high schools, colleges, etc.
7. Provide information and classes on rape prevention tactics.

If you want to obtain comprehensive materials about starting your own rape crisis center, please contact the following groups:

Rape Crisis Center
P.O. Box 21005
Washington, D.C. 20009
Ask for "How to Start a Rape Crisis Center" ($4.75)

Women's Crisis Center
211½ N. 4th Ave.
Ann Arbor, Michigan 48104
Send for "How to Organize a Women's Crisis Center" ($2.00)

W.O.A.R.
1220 Sansom St., 11th Floor
Philadelphia Pa. 19107
The Philadelphia Women Organized Against Rape have made their entire training sessions packet available. The cost of the training packet is $10.00

Bibliography

Amir, Menachim. *Patterns of Forcible Rape*. Urbana, Ill.: University of Chicago Press, 1971.

Brasch, R. *How Did Sex Begin?*. New York: David McKay Co., 1973.

Collier, James. *The Hypocritical American*. New York: The Bobbs-Merrill Co., 1964.

Griffin, Susan. "Rape: The All-American Crime." *Ramparts* 26–35, Sept., 1971.

The Institute for Sex Research. *Sex Offenders*. New York: Harper & Row., 1965.

Lear, Martha Weinman. "Q. If You Rape a Woman and Steal her TV, What Can They Get You for in New York? A. Stealing her TV." *New York Times Magazine* pp. 11, 55–62, Jan. 30, 1972.

MacDonald, John M. *Rape: Offenders and Their Victims*. Springfield, Ill.: Charles C. Thomas, 1971.

Marcus, Anthony M. *Nothing is my Number*. Toronto: General Publishing Co., 1971.

Massey, Joe B. "Management of Sexually Assaulted Females." *Obstetrics and Gynecology* 38:190–92, 1971.

Taylor, G. Rattray. *Sex in History*. New York: Vanguard Press, 1970.

Webster, William H. *Uniform Crime Reports*, U.S.

Dept. of Justice, Federal Bureau of Investigation, Washington, D.C., 1977 and 1978.

Wolfgang, Marvin, E. *Sexual Behaviors*. Boston: Little, Brown and Co., 1972.

A Directory of Multi-service Women's Centers

The Women's Action Alliance, founded in 1971, is a national center on women's issues and programs. Firmly committed to full equality for all persons, regardless of sex, the Alliance develops, coordinates, assists, and administers programs which will achieve this goal. Through its diverse services and projects, the Alliance accomplishes this by:

- Offering a national information and referral service;

- Developing technical assistance, publications, and projects in areas the Alliance identifies as major needs among women's organizations and in which we can offer expertise and resources;

- Promoting coalition-building among women's groups at the national and local levels;

- Providing leadership in eliminating sex-role conditioning in early childhood education.

370 Lexington Avenue, Room 603 New York, NY 10017 (212) 532-8330

For a free copy of the *National Directory of Rape Prevention and Treatment Resources*, write to the National Center for Prevention and Control of Rape, 5600 Fishers Lane, Rockville, MD 20857. If additional copies are desired, they must be purchased from the Government Printing Office.

The following nationwide list of multi-service women's centers was prepared by Women's Action Alliance. These centers provide referrals to health care services of many kinds.

ALASKA

Women in Crisis, Inc.
331 5th Ave.
Fairbanks, AK 99701

ARIZONA

Flagstaff Women's
Resource Center
3 N. Leroux St., Rm. 201
Flagstaff, AZ 86001

Center for Women
Phoenix College
1202 W. Thomas Rd.
Phoenix, AZ 85013

ASUA Women's Drop-In
Center
University of Arizona
Student Union 106
Tucson, AZ

Tucson Center for Women
& Children
419 S. Stone Ave.
Tucson, AZ 85701

CALIFORNIA

Berkeley Women's Center
2955 Telegraph Ave.
Berkeley, CA 94705

Center for Women & Religion
Graduate Theological
Union
2465 Le Conte
Berkeley, CA 94709

University of California
Women's Center
7-9 U.C.
Berkeley, CA 94720

Women's Center
Compton College
1111 E. Artesia Blvd.
Compton, CA 90221

Women's Resources &
Research Center
University of California
TB 116
Davis, CA 95616

California State University
Women's Center
LH 209
Fullerton, CA 92634

South County Women's
Center
25036 Carlos Bee Boulevard
Hayward, CA 94542

Women's Referral Center
Student Union Bldg.
California State University
1250 Bellflower Blvd.
Long Beach, CA 90840

Chicana Service Action
   Center
2244 Beverly Blvd.
Los Angeles, CA 90057

Women's Community, Inc.
The Women's Bldg.
1727 N. Spring St.
Los Angeles, CA 90012

Women's Resource Center
2 Dodd Hall
UCLA
Los Angeles, CA 90024

Women's Studies Center
Saddleback College
28000 Marguerite Pkwy.
Mission Viejo, CA 92692

ICI - A Woman's Place
5251 Broadway
Oakland, CA 94618

Resource Center for
   Women
445 Sherman Ave.
Palo Alto, CA 94306

YWCA
4161 Alma St.
Palo Alto, CA 94306

YWCA Women's Resource
   Center
16 E. Olive
Redlands, CA 92373

Sacramento Community for
   Women
2015 J St., Suite 30
Sacramento, CA 95814

Sacramento Women's Cen-
   ter & Bookstore
2104 Capitol Ave.
Sacramento, CA 95814

UCSB Women's Center
Santa Barbara, CA 91306

Center for Women's
   Studies & Services
908 F St.
San Diego, CA 92101

San Francisco Women's
   Centers
3543 18th St.
San Francisco, CA 94110

Women's Center of S.F.
   State U.
1600 Holloway
San Francisco, CA 94132

San Jose State University
   Women's Center
177 S. 10th St.
San Jose, CA 95152

WOMA - The Women's Al-
   liance
1509 E. Santa Clara St.
San Jose, CA 95116

San Luis Obispo Women's
   Resource Center
738 D-Higuera
San Luis Obispo, CA 93401

YWCA-Marin County
   Center
1648 Mission Ave.
San Rafael, CA

COLORADO

Virginia Neal Blue
  Women's Center
Adams State College Center
Room 207E
Alamosa, CO 81101

Boulder County Women's
  Resource Center
1406 Pine
Boulder, CO 80302

Women's Studies Program
#7 Hillside Ct.
University of Colorado
Boulder, CO 80302

Research Center on
  Women
Loretto Heights College
3001 S. Federal Blvd.
Denver, CO 80236

Virginia Neal Blue
  Resource Centers for
  Colorado Women
Colorado Women's College
Box 294
Denver, CO 80220

Woman to Woman
2023 E. Colfax
Denver, CO 80439

CONNECTICUT

Women's Center
Asnuntuck Community College
Box 68, 111 Phoenix Ave.
Enfield, CT 06082

Hartford Women's Center
57 Pratt St., Suite 301
Hartford, CT 06103

Trinity College Women's
  Center
Box 1385, Trinity College
Hartford, CT 06106

Manchester Community
  College Women's Center
50 Bidwell St.
Manchester, CT 06040

Wesleyan Women's Coalition
Box WW, Wesleyan University
Middletown, CT 06457

Prudence Crandall Center
  for Women
37 Bassett St.
New Britain, CT 06050

Information & Counseling
  Service for Women
301 Crown St.
New Haven, CT 06520

New Haven Women's
  Liberation Center
148 Orange St.
New Haven, CT 06520

Women's Center of S.E.
  Conn., Inc.
120 Broad St., PO Box 172
New London, CT 06320

Counseling Center for
  Women
333 Wilson Ave.
Norwalk, CT 06854

Women's Center
University of Connecticut
27 Whitney Rd.
Storrs, CT 06268

Women's Representative
200 Bloomfield Ave.
West Hartford, CT 06117

DELAWARE

YWCA of New Castle
County
908 King St.
Wilmington, DE 19801

DISTRICT OF
COLUMBIA

Counseling & Career Center
ter
Trinity College
Washington, D.C. 20017

Washington Women's Art
Center
1821 Q St. NW
Washington, D.C. 20009

Womenspace
Marvin Center #430
800 21st St. NW
Washington, D.C. 20052

FLORIDA

Women's Walk-In Counseling Service
311 Little Hall
University of Florida
Gainesville, FL 32611

YWCA
1417 N. 12th Ave.
Pensacola, FL 32503

Domestic Assault Shelter
YWCA
901 S. Olive
West Palm Beach, FL
33401

GEORGIA

Feminist Action Alliance,
Inc. PO Box 54717
Civic Center Station
Atlanta, GA 30308

HAWAII

University YWCA
Women's Center
1820 University Ave.
Honolulu, HI 96822

IDAHO

Women's Resource Center
720 Washington
Boise, ID 83669

Women's Center
University of Idaho
Moscow, ID 83843

Women's Center
544 N. Garfield
Pocatello, ID 83201

ILLINOIS

Women's Center
408 W. Freeman
Carbondale, IL 62901

Ecumenical Women's Center
1653 W. School St.
Chicago, IL 60657

Midwest Women's Center
53 Jackson Blvd., Rm. 623
Chicago, IL 60604

University Feminist Organization
University of Chicago
5655 S. University Ave.
Chicago, IL 60637

YWCA
436 N. Main
Decatur, IL 62501

Evanston Women's Liberation Center
2214 Ridge Ave.
Evanston, IL 60201

Women at Northwestern
619 Emerson St.
Evanston, IL 60201

YWCA Women's Center
541 W. Stephenson St.
Freeport, IL 61032

Women in Leadership Learning
Barat College
Lake Forest, IL 60045

Women's Program
Oakton Community College
7900 N. Nagle
Morton Grove, IL 60053

South Suburban Area YWCA
45 Plaza
Park Forest, IL 60466

Sojourn Women's Center
PO Box 1052
Springfield, IL 62705

WIRE (Women's Information & Resource Exchange)
1203 W. Green
Urbana, IL 61801

INDIANA

YWCA Women's Resource Center
122 W. Lexington Ave.
Elkhart, IN 46514

Fort Wayne Women's Bureau, Inc.
PO Box 554
Fort Wayne, IN 46807

Calumet Women United Against Rape
PO Box 2617
Gary, IN 46403

Women Alive!
229 Ogden St.
Box 1121
Hammond, IN 46325

Everywoman's Center
6354 W. 37th St.
Indianapolis, IN 46224

YWCA
4460 Guion Rd.
Indianapolis, IN 46254

YWCA Women's Center
802 N. Lafayette Blvd.
South Bend, IN 46601

IOWA

Women's Resource & Action Center
130 N. Madison St.
Iowa City, IA

Center for Women
3303 Rebecca
Sioux City, IA 51104

KANSAS

Women's Resource Center
Kansas State University
Manhattan, KS 66506

KENTUCKY

Alternatives for Women
1628 S. Limestone
Lexington, KY 40503

Women's Center
Brescia College
120 W. Seventh
Owensboro, KY 42301

LOUISIANA

The Women's Center for
Greater New Orleans
6322 Cromwell Pl., Box 36
Loyola University
New Orleans, LA 70118

MAINE

University Women's Forum
94 Bedford St.
Portland, ME 04106

MARYLAND

YWCA Women's Center
167 Duke of Gloucester St.
Annapolis, MD 21401

Baltimore New Directions
for Women
2517 N. Charles
Baltimore, MD 21218

Women's Growth Center
339 E. 25th St.
Baltimore, MD 21218

Women Together
5609 Cross County Blvd.
Baltimore, MD 21209

New Responses, Inc.
6509 Westland Rd.
Bethesda, MD 20034

Resources for Women
4422 Walsh St.
Chevy Chase, MD 20015

Women's Center
Towson State University
Towson, MD 21204

MASSACHUSETTS

Everywoman's Center
Wilder Hall, 2nd Fl.
University of Massachusetts
Amherst, MA 01002

Widening Opportunities
Research Center
Middlesex Community College
Box 1
Bedford, MA 01730

Boston University Women's Center
775 Commonwealth Ave.
Boston, MA 02115

Women's Information & Referral Education Services
117 Newbury St.
Boston, MA 02116

Center for Women at Massasoit
Massasoit Community College
290 Thatcher St.
Brockton, MA 02402

Cambridge YWCA
7 Temple St.
Cambridge, MA 02139

Women's Counseling & Resource Center
1555 Massachusetts Ave.
Cambridge, MA 02139

Women's Educational Center
46 Pleasant St.
Cambridge, MA 02139

Women's Center
Bristol Community College
64 Durfee St.
Fall River, MA 02720

YWCA Women's Resource Center
90 Irving St.
Framingham, MA 01701

Mercy Otis Warren Women's Center
298 Main St.
Hyannis, MA 02601

Greater Lawrence YWCA
38 Lawrence
Lawrence, MA 01840

L.M.S.C. Women's Center
26 Main St.
Leominster, MA 01453

New Bedford Women's Center, Inc.
15 Chestnut St.
New Bedford, MA 02740

The Women's Resource Center of Andover Theological School
215 Herrick Rd.
Newton Center, MA 02159

Women's Services Center
33 Pearl St.
Pittsfield, MA 01201

Women's Center
Quincy Junior College
34 Coddington St.
Quincy, MA 02169

Aswalos House YWCA
246 Seaver St.
Roxbury, MA 02121

Women's Inner-city Educational Resource Service, Inc. (Winners)
134 Warren St.
Roxbury, MA 02119

Origins
169 Boston St.
Salem, MA 01970

Somerville Women's Center
7 Davis Sq.
Somerville, MA 02144

Women's Resource Room
Watertown Multi-Service
   Center
465 Arsenal St.
Watertown, MA 02172

MICHIGAN

Ann Arbor Women's Crisis
   Center
211½ N. Fourth Ave.
Ann Arbor, MI 48104

Center for Continuing Education of Women
382-330 Thompson St.
Ann Arbor, MI 48109

Women's Center
Wayne State University
167 Mackenzie
Detroit, MI 48202

Women's Resource Center
226 Bostwick
Grand Rapids, MI 45903

Women's Resource Center
Schoolcraft College
18600 Haggerty Rd.
Livonia, MI 48152

Everywoman's Place, Inc.
23 Strong Ave.
Muskegon, MI 49441

MINNESOTA

Chrysalis, A Center for
   Women
2104 Stevens Ave. South
Minneapolis, MN 55404

Minnesota Women's Center
306 Walter Library
University of Minnesota
Minneapolis, MN 55455

Twin Cities Woman
430 Oak Grove St., B-10
Minneapolis, MN 55403

YWCA of the Minneapolis
   Area
1130 Nicollet Mall
Minneapolis, MN 55403

St. Cloud Area Women's
   Center
1900 Minnesota Blvd.
St. Cloud, MN 56301

Women's Advocates
584 Grand Ave.
St. Paul, MN 55102

Women's Information Line
Council on the Economic
   Status of Women
State Office
St. Paul, MN 55155

MISSOURI

New Directions Center
Columbia Public Schools
200 Austin
Columbia, MO 65201

The Family Self-Help Center
PO Box 1185
Joplin, MO 64801

Women's Center
University of Missouri - St.
  Louis
8001 Natural Bridge Rd.
St. Louis, MO 63121

MONTANA

Women's Center
146 E. 6th Ave.
Helena, MT 59601

Women's Place
1130 W. Broadway
Missoula, MT 59801

Women's Resource Center
University Center
University of Montana
Missoula, MT 59801

NEBRASKA

Women's Study Group
Doane College
Crete, NE 68508

Women's Resource Center
Room 116
14 & R Sts. Nebraska Union
Lincoln, NE 68508

YWCA Women's Resource
  Center
1432 N St.
Lincoln, NE 68508

NEW HAMPSHIRE

Women's Supportive Services
94 Sullivan St.
Claremont, NH 03743

Women's Information Service (Wise)
38 S. Main
Hanover, NH 03755

Women's Center
YWCA
40 Merrimac St.
Portsmouth, NH 03801

NEW JERSEY

Union Center for Women
8101 Ridge Blvd.
Brooklyn, NJ 11209

Women's Center of Brooklyn College
3410 James Hall
Brooklyn, NJ 11210

Alternatives for Women
NOW
517 Penn St.
Camden, NJ 08102

Together, Inc.
7 State St.
Glassboro, NJ 08028

Women's Center
Jersey City State College
70 Audubon Ave.
Jersey City, NJ 07305

The Women's Advisory Exchange
11 Green Hill Rd.
Madison, NJ 07940

Women's Center/YWCA
15 W. Main St.
Moorestown, NJ 08057

YWCA Women's Center
185 Carroll St.
Paterson, NJ 07501

Women's Center for People
4 Waldron Ave.
Summit, NJ 07901

Women's Center of Unitarian House for People
Whittredge Rd.
Summit, NJ 07901

Women's Rights in Tenafly
PO Box 523
Tenafly, NJ 07670

NEW MEXICO

Women's Center
1824 Las Lomas, N.E.
University of New Mexico
Albuquerque, NM 87131

YWCA Women's Resource Center
316 4th St., S.W.
Albuquerque, NM 87102

NEW YORK

Lesbian Switchboard
PO Box 354
Binghamton, NY 13902

Women's Center & Rape Crisis Center
56-58 Whitney Ave.
Binghamton, NY 13902

Women's Action Coalition/Women's Resource Center
Campus Center, SUC Fredonia
Fredonia, NY 14063

Women's Liberation Center of Nassau County
2570 Hempstead Tpk.
East Meadow, NY 11544

Womanspace in Great Neck
70 Grace Ave.
Great Neck, NY 11021

Women's Center
Hofstra University Student Center
Hempstead, NY 11551

Women's Resource Center of the Jamestown Girls Club, Inc.
532 E. Second St.
Jamestown, NY 14701

Women's Information Center
Keuka College
Keuka Park, NY 14478

Westchester Women's Center
W. 2nd St. & S. 6th Ave.
Mt. Vernon, NY 10550

Barnard Women's Center
Barnard College
New York, NY 10027

International Women's Year Tribune
345 E. 46th St., Rm. 815
New York, NY 10017

Women's Center/Riverside
490 Riverside Dr., Rm. 520,
   South Wing
New York, NY 10027

Young Women's Christian
   Association
610 Lexington Ave.
New York, NY 10022

Islip Women's Center
855 Montauk Hwy.
Oakdale, NY 11796

Oswego Women Center
207 Hewitt Union Bldg.,
   SUCO
Oswego, NY 13126

Nassau County Office of
   Women's Services
1425 Old Country Rd.
Plainview, NY 11803

The Feminist Union
Vassar College, Box 172
Poughkeepsie, NY 12601

Riverdale Neighborhood
   House
5521 Mosholu Ave.
Riverdale, NY 10471

New Directions Resource
   Center of Southampton
   College
Abney Peak
Southampton, NY 11968

The Women's Center
Syracuse University
750 Ostrom
Syracuse, NY 13210

Women's Information Cen-
   ter
601 Allen St.
Syracuse, NY 13210

WomanKind
c/o Jean Whelan
119 Ward St.
Westbury, NY 11590

The Women's Center of
   Yonkers
291 Palisade Ave.
Commerce Community
   Center, Rm. 218
Yonkers, NY 10701

NORTH CAROLINA

A Woman's Place
110 Henderson St. (POB
   509)
Chapel Hill, NC 27514

Durham Women's Center
YWCA
312 E. Umstead St.
Durham, NC 27707

The Council on
   Appalachian Women
Box 490
Mars Hill, NC 28754

NORTH DAKOTA

Office of Women's Pro-
   grams
Box 326
University of North Dakota
Grand Forks, ND 58202

OHIO

Women's Network
39 E. Market St., Suite
  #502
Akron, OH 44308

Athens Women's Collective
Baker Center
Ohio University
Athens, OH 45701

Women's Programs & Serv-
  ices
Sander Plaza 1
University of Cincinnati
Cincinnati, OH 45221

WomenSpace
1258 Euclid Ave., #200
Cleveland, OH 44120

Women Together, Inc.
PO Box 6331
Cleveland, OH 44101

Dayton Women's Center
1309 N. Main St.
Dayton, OH 45405

Oberlin Women's Center
92 Spring St.
Oberlin, OH 44074

Project Women
712½ N. Fountain
Springfield, OH 45504

Antioch College Women's
  Center
Yellow Springs, OH 45387

OKLAHOMA

Women's Resource Center,
  Inc.
PO Box 474, 207½ E. Gray
Norman, OK 73069

YWCA of Oklahoma City
129 N.W. Fifth St.
Oklahoma City, OK 73102

YWCA Women's Resource
  Center
3626 North Western
Oklahoma City, OK 73118

Women's Center of Tulsa
1240 E. 5th Pl., Room 200
Tulsa, OK 74135

OREGON

Women's Resource Center
  of Lincoln City
908 SW Hurbert
Newport, OR 97365

Women's Place Resource
  Center
1915 NE Everett
Portland, OR 97232

PENNSYLVANIA

Women's Center of Mont-
  gomery County
1030 York Rd.
Abington, PA 19001

Women's Center
Cedar Crest College
Allentown, PA 18104

Women's Network, Inc.
107 E. Oakland Ave.
Doylestown, PA 18901

Villa Maria College
2551 West Lake Rd.
Erie, PA 16505

The Women's Center,
    YWCA
4th and Market
Harrisburg, PA 17101

Lancaster Women's Liberation
344 W. King
Lancaster, PA 17603

Womensplace
631 Shaw Ave.
McKeesport, PA 15132

Women's Information Service of Women's Action Coalition, POB 63
Media, PA 19063

Fishtown Women's Community Center
1340 Frankford Ave.
Philadelphia, PA 19125

Kensington Women's Center
YWCA
174 W. Allegheny
Philadelphia, PA 19133

Penn Women's Center
Houston Hall
University of Pennsylvania
Philadelphia, PA 19104

Women Against Abuse
PO Box 12233
Philadelphia, PA 19144

Women's Center & Shelter of Greater Pittsburgh
616 N. Highland Ave., Box 11
Pittsburgh, PA 15206

Women's Center
University of Pittsburgh
3802 Forbes Ave.
Pittsburgh, PA 15260

YWCA of Greater Pittsburgh
4th & Wood Sts.
Pittsburgh, PA 15222

Women's Resource Center
YWCA, 8th & Washington Sts.
Reading, PA 19601

Women's Resource Center, Inc.
312-15A Bank Towers Bldg.
Spruce St. & Wyoming Ave.
Scranton, PA 18503

Centre County Women's Resource Center
103 E. Beaver Ave., #6
State College, PA 16801

Women's Resource Center
PO Box 309
Wayne, PA 19087

YWCA Women's Center
42 W. Maiden St.
Washington, PA 15301

The Ina C. Braden Center for Women
Community College of Allegheny County
South Campus
1750 Clairton Rd.
W. Mifflin, PA 15122

RHODE ISLAND

Kingston Women's Liberation
Memorial Union
University of Rhode Island
Kingston, RI 02881

Sarah Doyle Women's Center
PO Box 1829, 185 Meeting St.
Providence, RI 02912

Women's Center, Inc.
37 Congress Ave.
Providence, RI 02907

SOUTH DAKOTA

Brookings Women's Center
802 11th Ave.
Brookings, SD 57006

TENNESSEE

Knoxville Women's Center
406 Church St.
Knoxville, TN 37902

Women's Resources Center
499 S. Patterson St.
Memphis, TN 38111

Vanderbilt University Women's Center
E-2 W. Side Row
Box 1513-B
Nashville, TN 37235

TEXAS

The Austin Women's Center
711 San Antonio
Austin, TX 78701

Everywoman's Center
Richland College
12800 Abrams Rd.
Dallas, TX 75243

Women's Center of Dallas
2800 Routh, Suite 197
Dallas, TX 75201

YWCA Women's Resource Center
1600 N. Brown
El Paso, TX 79936

Fort Worth Women's Center
1203 Lake St., Suite 208
Fort Worth, TX 76102

Houston Area Women's Center
PO Box 20186
Houston, TX 77025

UTAH

Weber State College Association for Status of Women
3750 Harrison Blvd.
Ogden, UT 84408

Phoenix Institute
383 S. 6th
Salt Lake City, UT

YWCA
322 E. 3rd South
Salt Lake City, UT 84111

VIRGINIA

Women's Resource Center/Ct. VA
Randolph-Macon Women's College
Lynchburg, VA 24503

ACLU Southern Women's Rights Project
1001 E. Main St., Suite 512
Richmond, VA 23219

Women's Resource & Service Center
YWCA Central Center
605 First St., S.W.
Roanoke, VA 24011

Williamsburg Area Women's Center
PO Box 126
Williamsburg, VA 23185

WASHINGTON

Eastside Community Mental Health Center
2253 140th NE
Bellevue, WA 98005

Women's Association of Self Help
11100 N.E. 2nd
PO Box 3023
Bellevue, WA 98099

Women's Center
Western Washington University
V.U. 215, Western Wash. Univ.
Bellingham, WA 98225

Asian Counseling & Referral Service, Inc.
655 S. Jackson
Seattle, WA 98104

Community Service Officer Sec.
1810 E. Yesler Way
Seattle, WA 98122

Crisis Clinic, Inc.
1530 Eastlake E.
Seattle, WA 98102

Open Door Clinic
5012 Roosevelt Way, NE
Seattle, WA 98105

University YWCA
4224 University Way, NE
Seattle, WA 98105

YWCA Women's Resource Center
1118 5th Ave.
Seattle, WA 98101

Women's Studies & Services
Ft. Steilacoom C.C.
9401 Farwest Dr., S.W.
Tacoma, WA 98498

YWCA Women's Resource Center
405 Broadway
Tacoma, WA 98409

WEST VIRGINIA

Shenandoah Women's Centers
PO Box 1083
Martinsburg, WV 25401

Women's Information Center
221 Willey St.
Morgantown, WV 26505

WISCONSIN

Lucy Stone Center for Women
University of Wisconsin
Green Bay, WI 54302

Women's Service Center
102 N. Monroe
Green Bay, WI 54301

Research Center on Women
Alverno College
3401 S. 39th
Milwaukee, WI 23515

UW-M Feminist Center
University of Wisconsin
Student Union, Box 189
Milwaukee, WI 53201

The Women's Coalition
2211 E. Kenwood Blvd.
Milwaukee, WI 53211

Women's Center
124 Blackhawk Commons
Oshkosh, WI 54901

Women's Resource Center
7436 Paul Bunyan Rd.
Racine, WI 53402

Women's Resource Center, Inc.
2101A Main St.
Stevens Point, WI 54481

The Women's Center, Inc.
419 N. Grand Ave.
Waukesha, WI 53186

WYOMING

Women's Self-Help Center
906 N. Durbin
Casper, WY 82601

PUERTO RICO

Centro de Ayuda a Victimas de Violacion
Anexo 4, Edificio A de Psiquiastria
Rio Piedras, Puerto Rico

CANADA

Status of Women Action Committee
320 5th Ave., S.E.
Calgary, Alberta

Women's Resource Centre
Women's Div., Dept. of Labour
T.D. Bldg., 5th Floor
1914 Hamilton St.
Regina, Saskatchewan

THE WOMEN'S LIBRARY

Women must take particular care of their bodies to stay healthy. Their medical and personal needs require a vigilance quite different from that of men and children. In spite of this fact, becoming pregnant, not becoming pregnant, rape, vaginal care and menstruation have for generations been subjects discussed only behind closed doors and in doctors' offices. Not surprisingly, myths and misconceptions flourished.

The Women's Library treats these topics openly and conversationally. The authors investigate the medical and personal options available to women and offer thoroughly researched recommendations. These are factual books that focus on how to make practical use of information about our bodies, how to determine which choice among many is best, and why. And, how to satisfy the curiosity women have by answering once-private questions.

PREPARED CHILDBIRTH
by Tarvez Tucker

This book offers a consideration of today's alternatives to traditional methods of childbirth. Women can learn to participate in childbirth through an understanding of labor, training, activity and the conscious control of discomfort.

MENSTRUATION
by Hilary C. Maddux

A guide to menstruation's effects on the lives of women and men. This book includes practical suggestions for preventing and coping with menstrual difficulties and the significance of menstruation in both personal and social relationships.

BIRTH CONTROL
by Tarvez Tucker

A woman's guide to every method of contraception. Descriptions of how each works, its effectiveness, correct use, side effects and cost. This book includes a perspective on how different methods suit different women's lives.

VAGINAL HEALTH
by Carol V. Horos

What every woman should know about daily vaginal care and the gynecological exam. This book discusses the nature, recognition, cause and treatment of problems ranging from minor infections to venereal diseases.

RAPE
by Carol V. Horos

A look at the men who rape and the women they attack. Where it happens, how it's done and why some men are driven to it. This book offers protective measures and a guide to what to do if you are raped.

At your local bookstore or use this handy coupon for ordering: